CLASSIC SERIES

Greatest
Humour Stories

Published by:

V&S PUBLISHERS

F-2/16, Ansari road, Daryaganj, New Delhi-110002
☎ 23240026, 23240027 • *Fax:* 011-23240028
Email: info@vspublishers.com • *Website:* www.vspublishers.com

Regional Office : Hyderabad
5-1-707/1, Brij Bhawan (Beside Central Bank of India Lane)
Bank Street, Koti, Hyderabad - 500 095
☎ 040-24737290
E-mail: vspublishershyd@gmail.com

Branch Office : Mumbai
Godown # 34 at The Model Co-Operative Housing, Society Ltd.,
"Sahakar Niwas", Ground Floor, Next to Sobo Central, Mumbai - 400 034
☎ 022-22098268
E-mail: vspublishersmum@gmail.com

Follow us on:

For any assistance sms **VSPUB** to **56161**

All books available at **www.vspublishers.com**

© Copyright: *V&S PUBLISHERS*
ISBN 978-93-505710-3-3
Edition 2014

The Copyright of this book, as well as all matter contained herein (including illustrations) rests with the Publishers. No person shall copy the name of the book, its title design, matter and illustrations in any form and in any language, totally or partially or in any distorted form. Anybody doing so shall face legal action and will be responsible for damages.

Printed at : Param Offseters, Okhla, New Delhi-110020

Publisher's Note

It has been our constant endeavour at the **V&S Publishers** to publish all kinds of books ranging from Fiction, Non-fiction, Storybooks, Children Encyclopaedias, to Self-Help, Science Books, Dictionaries, Grammar Books, Self-Development, Management Books, etc.

However, this is for the first time that we are venturing into the vast, rich and fathomless ocean of English Literature and have come up with a set *of ten storybooks called the Greatest Classic Series* authored by some of the greatest and eminent writers of the world. There is a lot to learn from their writing style, selection of plot, development and building of theme and suspense of the story, emphasis and presentation of characters, dialogues, working towards the climax of the story, presenting the climax, and then finally concluding the story.

Each these books are of about 200 pages containing around ten popular stories or more of renowned authors like Oscar Wilde, Ernest William Hornung, Guy de Maupassant, O. Henry, Saki, Washington Irving, Thomas Hardy, Charles Dickens, Jules Verne, Jack London, Mark Twain, Edgar Allen Poe, H.G.Wells, Ambrose Bierce, Amelia Edwards, Edith Wharton, Wilkie Collins and many more. The series is called The Greatest Classic Series as all the names of the books begin with the word, 'Greatest' like the Greatest Adventurous Stories, Greatest Detective Stories, Greatest Love Stories, Greatest Ghost Stories, and so on. Besides this, three of the ten books are exclusively on the Adventures of Sherlock Holmes, one of the best detectives the world has ever known written by none other than Sir Arthur Conan Doyle.

Besides the above mentioned characteristics, the books contain an introductory page before each story introducing the author, his brief life history, notable works and literary achievements. Each story has a set of word meanings on each page followed by an exercise meant exclusively aiming the school students to help them grasp the essence of the story easily and quickly.

These books are not only a boon for the school-going students, particularly studying in senior classes from the seventh standard till the twelfth, but are also a treasure trove for all those young and aspiring writers, voracious readers and lovers of English language and literature.

Each of these ten books focus on a theme, such as adventure, love, terror, humour, or supernatural happenings, and are so captivating and real to life that readers may find it difficult to choose from them and so it's better to pick the entire series.

Wishing you all a happy and enjoyable reading…

Contents

Publisher's Note	3
The Girl And The Graft	7
The Robe Of Peace	21
Bertie's Christmas Eve	29
Proof Of The Pudding	37
Babes In The Jungle	57
One Summer Night	71
The Ransom Of Red Chief	74
The Legend Of Sleepy Hollow	87
A Matter Of Sentiment	105
The Princess And The Puma	110
A Nose For The King	119
A Ramble In Aphasia	127
My Favourite Murder	141
A Bread And Butter Miss	150
A Night In New Arabia	157
The Baron Of Grogzwig	175
John Mortonson's Funeral	187
The Gold That Glittered	190

The Girl And The Graft
~ O. Henry

The other day I ran across my old friend Ferguson Pogue. Pogue is a *conscientious* grafter of the highest type. His headquarters is the Western Hemisphere, and his line of business is anything from speculating in town lots on the Great Staked Plains to selling wooden toys in Connecticut, made by *hydraulic pressure* from nutmegs ground to a pulp.

Now and then when Pogue has made a good haul he comes to New York for a rest. He says the jug of wine and loaf of bread and Thou in the wilderness business is about as much rest and pleasure to him as sliding down the bumps at Coney would be to President Taft. "Give me," says Pogue, "a big city for my vacation. Especially New York. I'm not much fond of New Yorkers, and Manhattan is about the only place on the globe where I don't find any."

While in the metropolis Pogue can always be found at one of two places. One is a little second-hand bookshop on Fourth Avenue, where he reads books about his hobbies, Mahometanism and taxidermy. I found him at the other - his hall bedroom in Eighteenth Street - where he sat in his stocking feet trying to pluck "The Banks of the Wabash" out of a small zither. Four years he has practised this tune without arriving near enough to cast the longest trout line to the water's edge. On the dresser lay a blued-steel Colt's forty-five and a tight roll of tens and twenties large enough around to belong to the spring rattlesnake-story class. A chambermaid with a room-cleaning air *fluttered* nearby in the hall, unable to enter or to flee, scandalised by the stocking feet, aghast at the Colt's, yet powerless, with her metropolitan instincts, to remove herself beyond the magic influence of the yellow-hued roll.

I sat on his trunk while Ferguson Pogue talked. No one could be franker or more candid in his conversation. Beside his expression the cry of Henry James for lacteal nourishment at the age of one month would have seemed like a Chaldean cryptogram. He told me stories of his profession with pride, for he considered it an art. And I was curious enough to ask him whether he had known any women who followed it.

Conscientious - *Just, Honest*
Hydraulic pressure - *The dynamic behaviour of fluids*
Fluttered - *Toss about*
Scandalised - *Defamed*

"Ladies?" said Pogue, with Western chivalry. "Well, not to any great extent. They don't amount to much in special lines of graft, because they're all so busy in general lines. What? Why, they have to. Who's got the money in the world? The men. Did you ever know a man to give a woman a dollar without any consideration? A man will shell out his dust to another man free and easy and gratis. But if he drops a penny in one of the machines run by the Madam Eve's Daughters' Amalgamated Association and the pineapple chewing gum don't fall out when he pulls the lever you can hear him kick to the superintendent four blocks away. Man is the hardest proposition a woman has to go up against. He's the low-grade one, and she has to work overtime to make him pay. Two times out of five she's salted. She can't put in **crushers** and costly machinery. He'd notice 'em and be onto the game. They have to pan out what they get, and it hurts their tender hands. Some of 'em are natural **sluice** troughs and can carry out $1,000 to the ton. The dry-eyed ones have to depend on signed letters, false hair, sympathy, the kangaroo walk, cowhide whips, ability to cook, sentimental juries, conversational powers, silk underskirts, ancestry, rouge, anonymous letters, violet sachet powders, witnesses, revolvers, pneumatic forms, carbolic acid, moonlight, cold cream and the evening newspapers."

"You are outrageous, Ferg," I said. "Surely there is none of this 'graft' as you call it, in a perfect and **harmonious** matrimonial union!"

"Well," said Pogue, "nothing that would justify you every time in calling Police Headquarters and ordering out the reserves and a vaudeville manager on a dead run. But it's this way: Suppose you're a Fifth Avenue millionaire, soaring high, on the right side of copper and cappers.

"You come home at night and bring a $9,000,000 diamond brooch to the lady who's staked your for a claim. You hand it over. She says, 'Oh, George!' and looks to see if it's backed. She comes up and kisses you. You've waited for it. You get it. All right. It's graft.

"But I'm telling you about Artemisia Blye. She was from Kansas and she suggested corn in all of its phases. Her hair was as yellow as the silk; her form was as tall and graceful as a stalk in the low grounds during a wet summer; her eyes were as big and startling as bunions, and green was her favorite color.

Crushers - *To press or squeeze with a force that destroys/deforms*
Sluice troughs - *To let out/drain water through a long, narrow, open receptacle*
Harmonious - *Melodious*

"On my last trip into the cool recesses of your *sequestered* city I met a human named Vaucross. He was worth - that is, he had a million. He told me he was in business on the street. 'A sidewalk merchant?' says I, sarcastic. 'Exactly,' says he, 'Senior partner of a paving concern.'

"I kind of took to him. For this reason, I met him on Broadway one night when I was out of heart, luck, tobacco and place. He was all silk hat, diamonds and front. He was all front. If you had gone behind him you would have only looked yourself in the face. I looked like a cross between Count Tolstoy and a June *lobster*. I was out of luck. I had - but let me lay my eyes on that dealer again.

"Vaucross stopped and talked to me a few minutes and then he took me to a high-toned restaurant to eat dinner. There was music, and then some Beethoven, and Bordelaise sauce, and *cussing* in French, and frangipangi, and some hauteur and cigarettes. When I am flush I know them places.

"I declare, I must have looked as bad as a magazine artist sitting there without any money and my hair all rumpled like I was booked to read a chapter from 'Elsie's School Days' at a Brooklyn Bohemian smoker. But Vaucross treated me like a bear hunter's guide. He wasn't afraid of hurting the waiter's feelings.

"'Mr. Pogue,' he explains to me, 'I am using you.'

"'Go on,' says I; 'I hope you don't wake up.'

"And then he tells me, you know, the kind of man he was. He was a New Yorker. His whole ambition was to be noticed. He wanted to be *conspicuous*. He wanted people to point him out and bow to him, and tell others who he was. He said it had been the desire of his life always. He didn't have but a million, so he couldn't attract attention by spending money. He said he tried to get into public notice one time by planting a little public square on the east side with garlic for free use of the poor; but Carnegie heard of it, and covered it over at once with a library in the Gaelic language. Three times he had jumped in the way of automibiles; but the only result was five broken ribs and a notice in the papers that an unknown man, five feet ten, with four amalgam-filled teeth, supposed to be the last of the famous Red Leary gang had been run over.

"'Ever try the reporters,' I asked him.

Sequestered - *Te remove/withdraw into solitude*
Lobster - *A large sized prawn*
Cussing - *Swearing, curseny*
Conspicuous - *Clearly, vividly*

"'Last month,' says Mr. Vaucross, 'my expenditure for lunches to reporters was $124.80.'

"'Get anything out of that?' I asks.

"'That reminds me,' says he; 'add $8.50 for perpsin. Yes, I got indigestion.'

"'How am I supposed to push along your scramble for prominence?' I inquires. 'Contrast?'

"'Something of that sort to-night,' says Vaucross. 'It grieves me; but I am forced to resort to *eccentricity*.' And here he drops his napkin in his soup and rises up and bows to a gent who is devastating a potato under a palm across the room.

"'The Police Commissioner,' says my climber, gratified. 'Friend', says I, in a hurry, 'have ambitions but don't kick a rung out of your ladder. When you use me as a stepping stone to salute the police you spoil my appetite on the grounds that I may be degraded and *incriminated*. Be thoughtful.'

"At the Quaker City squab en casserole the idea about Artemisia Blye comes to me.

"'Suppose I can manage to get you in the papers,' says I - 'a column or two every day in all of 'em and your picture in most of 'em for a week. How much would it be worth to you?' "'Ten thousand dollars,' says Vaucross, warm in a minute. 'But no murder,' says he; 'and I won't wear pink pants at a cotillon.'

"'I wouldn't ask you to,' says I. 'This is honourable, stylish and uneffiminate. Tell the waiter to bring a demi tasse and some other beans, and I will disclose to you the opus moderandi.' "We closed the deal an hour later in the rococo rouge et noise room. I telegraphed that night to Miss Artemisia in Salina. She took a couple of photographs and an autograph letter to an elder in the Fourth Presbyterian Church in the morning, and got some transportation and $80. She stopped in Topeka long enough to trade a flashlight interior and a valentine to the vice-president of a trust company for a mileage book and a package of five-dollar notes with $250 scrawled on the band.

"The fifth evening after she got my wire she was waiting, all decolletee and dressed up, for me and Vaucross to take her to dinner in one of these New York feminine apartment houses where a man can't get in unless he plays *bezique* and

Bezique - *A card game*
Incriminated - *Accused*
Eccentricity - *Madness, Craziness*

smokes depilatory powder cigarettes. "'She's a stunner,' says Vaucross when he saw her. 'They'll give her a two-column cut sure.' "This was the scheme the three of us concocted. It was business straight through. Vaucross was to rush Miss Blye with all the style and display and emotion he could for a month. Of course, that amounted to nothing as far as his ambitions were concerned. The sight of a man in a white tie and patent leather pumps pouring greenbacks through the large end of a **cornucopia** to purchase nutriment and hearts-ease for tall, **willowy blondes** in New York is as common a sight as blue turtles in delirium tremens. But he was to write her love letters - the worst kind of love letters, such as your wife publishes after you are dead - every day. At the end of the month he was to drop her, and she would bring suit for $100,000 for breach of promise.

"Miss Artemisia was to get $10,000. If she won the suit that was all; and if she lost she was to get it anyhow. There was a signed contract to that effect.

"Sometimes they had me out with 'em, but not often. I couldn't keep up to their style. She used to pull out his notes and criticize them like bills of lading.

"'Say, you!' she'd say. 'What do you call this - letter to a Hardware Merchant from His Nephew on Learning that His Aunt Has Nettlerash? You Eastern **duffers** know as much about writing love letters as a Kansas grasshopper does about **tugboats**. "My dear Miss Blye!" - wouldn't that put pink icing and a little red sugar bird on your bridal cake? How long do you expect to hold an audience in a court-room with that kind of stuff? You want to get down to business, and call me "Tweedlums Babe" and "Honeysuckle," and sing yourself "Mama's Own Big Bad Puggy Wuggy Boy" if you want any limelight to concentrate upon your **sparse** gray hairs. Get **sappy**.'

"After that Vaucross dipped his pen in the indelible tabasco. His notes read like something or other in the original. I could see a jury sitting up, and women tearing one another's hats to hear 'em read. And I could see piling up for Mr. Vaucross as much **notoriousness** as Archbishop Crammer or the Brooklyn Bridge or cheese-on-salad ever enjoyed. He seemed mighty pleased at the prospects.

"They agreed on a night; and I stood on Fifth Avenue outside a solemn restaurant and watched 'em. A process-server

Cornucoupla - *A horn containing atundant supply food, drink*
Willowy - *Slender, graceful*
Blodes - *Having fair hair and vsually fair skin and light eyes*
Duffers - *Plading, clumy person*
Tugboats - *Small, Powerful boats*

walked in and handed Vaucross the papers at this table. Everybody looked at 'em; and he looked as proud as Cicero. I went back to my room and lit a five-cent cigar, for I knew the $10,000 was as good as ours.

"About two hours later somebody knocked at my door. There stood Vaucross and Miss Artemisia, and she was clinging - yes, sir, clinging - to his arm. And they tells me they'd been out and got married. And they **articulated** some trivial **cadences** about love and such. And they laid down a bundle on the table and said 'Good night' and left.

"And that's why I say," concluded Ferguson Pogue, "that a woman is too busy occupied with her natural vocation and instinct of graft such as is given her for self-preservation and amusement to make any great success in special lines."

"What was in the bundle they left?" I asked, with my usual curiosity.

"Why," said Ferguson, "there was a scalper's railroad ticket as far as Kansas City and two pairs of Mr. Vaucross's old pants."

Food For Thought

Why do you think Miss Artemisia choose vaucrossas her husband instead of Ferguson pogue? Explain your answer with appropriate reasons.

Articulated - *Made clear or distinct*
Caences - *Arhythmic pattern of sounds/ beats*
Amusement - *Recreation, enjoyment*

An Understanding

Q. 1. What experiences did Ferguson Pogue narrate to the narrator or speaker about his profession of preparing and selling wooden toys?
Ans. _____
_____
_____
_____
_____

Q. 2. Where did Poge enjoy spending his vacation and why?
Ans. _____
_____
_____
_____
_____

Q. 3. What humour elements do you find in the story when Pogue describes the ways in which he and vaucross, including others in his company tried to woo and please Miss Artemisia Blye?
Ans. _____
_____
_____
_____
_____

Q. 4. "And that's why I say," concluded Ferguson Pogue, "that a woman is too busy occupied with her instinct of graft, such as is given to her for self - preservation and amusement to make any great success in special lines." Why does Pogue say these words to the narrator? What does he mean by saying so?
Ans. _____
_____
_____
_____
_____

Canossa

– Saki

DEmosthenes Platterbaff, the eminent Unrest Inducer, stood on his trial for a serious offence, and the eyes of the political world were focussed on the jury. The offence, it should be stated, was serious for the Government rather than for the prisoner. He had blown up the Albert Hall on the eve of the great Liberal Federation Tango Tea, the occasion on which the Chancellor of the Exchequer was expected to propound his new theory: "Do **partridges** spread infectious diseases?" Platterbaff had chosen his time well; the Tango Tea had been hurriedly postponed, but there were other political fixtures which could not be put off under any circumstances. The day after the trial there was to be a by-election at Nemesis-on-Hand, and it had been openly announced in the division that if Platterbaff were languishing in gaol on polling day the Government candidate would be "outed" to a certainty. Unfortunately, there could be no doubt or **misconception** as to Platterbaff's guilt.

He had not only pleaded guilty, but had expressed his intention of repeating his escapade in other directions as soon as circumstances permitted; throughout the trial he was busy examining a small model of the Free Trade Hall in Manchester. The jury could not possibly find that the prisoner had not deliberately and intentionally blown up the Albert Hall; the question was: Could they find any extenuating circumstances which would permit of an acquittal? Of course any sentence which the law might feel compelled to inflict would be followed by an immediate pardon, but it was highly desirable, from the Government's point of view, that the necessity for such an exercise of clemency should not arise. A **headlong** pardon, on the eve of a by-election, with threats of a heavy voting defection if it were withheld or even delayed, would not necessarily be a surrender, but it would look like one. **Opponents** would be only too ready to attribute ungenerous motives. Hence the anxiety in the crowded Court, and in the little groups gathered round the tape-machines in Whitehall and Downing Street and other affected centres.

The jury returned from considering their verdict; there was a flutter, an excited murmur, a death-like **hush**. The foreman delivered his message:

"The jury find the prisoner guilty of blowing up the Albert Hall. The jury wish to add a rider drawing attention to the fact

Partridges - *Small old world game birds*
Headlong - *Without delay, hastily, plunge*
Misconception - *False notion*
Opponents - *Competitions*

that a by-election is pending in the Parliamentary division of Nemesis-on-Hand."

"That, of course," said the Government Prosecutor, springing to his feet, "is equivalent to an *acquittal*?"

"I hardly think so," said the Judge, coldly; "I feel obliged to sentence the prisoner to a week's imprisonment."

"And may the Lord have mercy on the poll," a Junior Counsel exclaimed irreverently. It was a scandalous sentence, but then the Judge was not on the Ministerial side in politics. The verdict and sentence were made known to the public at twenty minutes past five in the afternoon; at half-past five a dense crowd was ***massed*** outside the Prime Minister's residence lustily singing, to the air of "Trelawney":

> "And should our Hero rot in gaol,
>
> For e'en a single day,
>
> There's Fifteen Hundred Voting Men
>
> Will vote the other way."

"Fifteen hundred," said the Prime Minister, with a shudder; "it's too horrible to think of. Our majority last time was only a thousand and seven."

"The poll opens at eight to-morrow morning," said the Chief Organiser; "we must have him out by 7 a.m."

"Seven-thirty," amended the Prime Minister; "we must avoid any appearance of precipitancy."

"Not later than seven-thirty, then," said the Chief Organiser; "I have promised the agent down there that he shall be able to display posters announcing 'Platterbaff is Out,' before the poll opens. He said it was our only chance of getting a telegram 'Radprop is In' to-night."

At half-past seven the next morning the Prime Minister and the Chief Organiser sat at breakfast, making a perfunctory meal, and awaiting the return of the Home Secretary, who had gone in person to superintend, the releasing of Platterbaff. Despite the earliness of the hour a small crowd had gathered in the street outside, and the horrible ***menacing*** Trelawney ***refrain*** of the "Fifteen Hundred Voting Men" came in a steady, ***monotonous*** chant.

"They will cheer presently when they hear the news," said the Prime Minister hopefully; "hark! They are ***booing*** some one now! That must be McKenna."

The Home Secretary entered the room a moment later, disaster written on his face.

"He won't go!" he exclaimed.

Acquittal - *The deliverance/release a person before a court*
Massed - *Heap/Pile*
Menacing - *Extremely annoying person*
Refrainent - *Desist, Forbear*
Monotonous - *Boring, dull*

Greatest Humour Stories

"Won't go? Won't leave gaol?"

"He won't go unless he has a brass band. He says he never has left prison without a brass band to play him out, and he's not going to go without one now."

"But surely that sort of thing is provided by his supporters and admirers?" said the Prime Minister; "we can hardly be supposed to supply a released prisoner with a brass band. How on earth could we defend it on the Estimates?"

"His supporters say it is up to us to provide the music," said the Home Secretary; "they say we put him in prison, and it's our affair to see that he leaves it in a respectable manner. Anyway, he won't go unless he has a band."

The telephone **squealed shrilly**; it was a trunk call from Nemesis.

"Poll opens in five minutes. Is Platterbaff out yet? In Heaven's name, why --"

The Chief Organiser rang off.

"This is not a moment for standing on dignity," he observed **bluntly**; "musicians must be supplied at once. Platterbaff must have his band."

"Where are you going to find the musicians?" asked the Home Secretary **wearily**; "we can't employ a military band, in fact, I don't think he'd have one if we offered it, and there ain't any others. There's a musicians' strike on, I suppose you know."

"Can't you get a strike permit?" asked the Organiser.

"I'll try," said the Home Secretary, and went to the telephone.

Eight o'clock struck. The crowd outside chanted with an increasing volume of sound:

"Will vote the other way."

A telegram was brought in. It was from the central committee rooms at Nemesis. "Losing twenty votes per minute," was its brief message.

Ten o'clock struck. The Prime Minister, the Home Secretary, the Chief Organiser, and several earnest helpful friends were gathered in the inner gateway of the prison, talking volubly to Demosthenes Platterbaff, who stood with folded arms and squarely planted feet, silent in their midst. Golden-tongued legislators whose **eloquence** had **swayed** the Marconi Inquiry Committee, or at any rate the greater part of it, expended their arts of oratory in vain on this stubborn

Booing - *To shout and express disgust*
Bluntly - *Rudely*
Squaled - *Sudden violent gust of wind*
Shrilly - *High pitched voice*
Wearily - *Tiredly*

unyielding man. Without a band he would not go; and they had no band.

A quarter past ten, half-past. A constant stream of telegraph boys poured in through the prison gates.

"Yamley's factory hands just voted you can guess how," ran a despairing message, and the others were all of the same *tenour*. Nemesis was going the way of Reading.

"Have you any band instruments of an easy nature to play?" demanded the Chief Organiser of the Prison Governor; "drums, *cymbals*, those sort of things?"

"The warders have a private band of their own," said the Governor, "but of course I couldn't allow the men themselves --"

"Lend us the instruments," said the Chief Organiser.

One of the earnest helpful friends was a skilled performer on the cornet, the Cabinet Ministers were able to clash cymbals more or less in tune, and the Chief Organiser has some knowledge of the drum.

"What tune would you prefer?" he asked Platterbaff.

"The popular song of the moment," replied the Agitator after a moment's reflection. It was a tune they had all heard hundreds of times, so there was no difficulty in turning out a *passable* imitation of it. To the improvised strains of "I didn't want to do it" the prisoner strode forth to freedom. The word of the song had reference, it was understood, to the incarcerating Government and not to the destroyer of the Albert Hall.

The seat was lost, after all, by a narrow majority. The local Trade Unionists took offence at the fact of Cabinet Ministers having personally acted as strike-breakers, and even the release of Platterbaff failed to pacify them. The seat was lost, but Ministers had scored a moral victory. They had shown that they knew when and how to *yield.*

Eloquence - *Ease in using language to the best effect*
Swayed - *To move or swing to one side or in one direction*
Tenor - *Period*
Cymbals - *Percussion instruments of indefinite pitch*
Passable - *Adequate, acceptable*

Food For Thought

Why do you think the Prime Minister released Platterbaff from jail and also asked the Brass Band to play him out? The Cabinet Ministers and the Prime Minister lost the elections but won the people's hearts. Do you agree? Support your answer with relevant reasons.

An Understanding

Q. 1. What was the offence of Demosthenes Platterbaff, the eminent Unrest Induces?
Ans. _____
_____
_____
_____
_____

Q. 2. Why has the author, Saki (H.H.Munro) named the story as 'Canossa'? What does it mean and how does it go with the story?
Ans. _____
_____
_____
_____
_____

Q. 3. The jury couldnot find that the guilty, Platterbaff, who was also the prisoner intentionally blew up the Albert Hall. How did then they found the circumstances that would permit of an acquittal?
Ans. _____
_____
_____
_____
_____

Q. 4. The verdict was passed that Platter baff was found guilty of blowing up the Albert Hall and was sentenced to a week's imprisonment. What was the reaction of the public after this announcement?
Ans. _____
_____
_____
_____
_____

The Robe Of Peace
~ O. Henry

MYsteries follow one another so closely in a great city that the reading public and the friends of Johnny Bellchambers have ceased to marvel at his sudden and unexplained disappearance nearly a year ago. This particular mystery has now been cleared up, but the solution is so strange and *incredible* to the mind of the average man that only a select few who were in close touch with Bellchambers will give it full *credence*.

Johnny Bellchambers, as is well known, belonged to the intrinsically inner circle of the *elite*. Without any of the ostentation of the fashionable ones who endeavor to attract notice by eccentric display of wealth and show he still was *au fait* in everything that gave deserved *lustre* to his high position in the ranks of society.

Especially did he shine in the matter of dress. In this he was the despair of *imitators*. Always correct, *exquisitely* groomed, and possessed of an unlimited wardrobe, he was conceded to be the best-dressed man in New York, and, therefore, in America. There was not a tailor in Gotham who would not have deemed it a precious boon to have been granted the privilege of making Bellchambers' clothes without a cent of pay. As he wore them, they would have been a priceless advertisement.

Trousers were his special passion. Here nothing but perfection would he notice. He would have worn a patch as quickly as he would have overlooked a wrinkle. He kept a man in his apartments always busy pressing his *ample* supply. His friends said that three hours was the limit of time that he would wear these garments without exchanging.

Bellchambers disappeared very suddenly. For three days his absence brought no alarm to his friends, and then they began to operate the usual methods of inquiry. All of them failed. He had left absolutely no trace behind. Then the search

Incredible - *Extraordinary*
Credence - *Acceptance or belief*
Elite - *Person of the highest class*
Lustre - *Sheen*
Imitators - *Copy, follow*
Exquisitely - *Of special beauty/charm*
Ample - *Enough*

for a motive was instituted, but none was found. He had no enemies, he had no debts, there was no woman.

There were several thousand dollars in his bank to his credit. He had never showed any tendency toward mental eccentricity; in fact, he was of a particularly calm and well-balanced *temperament*. Every means of tracing the vanished man was made use of, but without avail. It was one of those cases - more numerous in late years - where men seem to have gone out like the flame of a candle, leaving not even a trail of smoke as a witness.

In May, Tom Eyres and Lancelot Gilliam, two of Bellchambers' old friends, went for a little run on the other side. While *pottering* around in Italy and Switzerland, they happened, one day, to hear of a monastery in the Swiss Alps that promised something outside of the ordinary tourist-*beguiling* attractions. The monastery was almost inaccessible to the average sightseer, being on an extremely rugged and precipitous spur of the mountains. The attractions it possessed but did not advertise were, first, an exclusive and divine *cordial* made by the monks that was said to far surpass benedictine and chartreuse.

Next a huge brass bell so purely and accurately cast that it had not ceased sounding since it was first rung three hundred years ago. Finally, it was asserted that no Englishman had ever set foot within its walls. Eyres and Gilliam decided that these three reports called for investigation.

It took them two days with the aid of two guides to reach the monastery of St. Gondrau. It stood upon a frozen, windswept crag with the snow piled about it in treacherous, drifting masses. They were hospitably received by the brothers whose duty it was to entertain the infrequent guest. They drank of the precious cordial, finding it rarely potent and reviving. They listened to the great, ever-echoing bell, and learned that they were pioneer travelers, in those gray stone walls, over the Englishman whose restless feet have trodden nearly every corner of the earth.

Pacing - *The rate of movement*
Treading - *Walking or Trampling*
Temperament - *Attitude/Nature*
Pottering - *Making pottery*
Beguiling - *To influence by trickery/flattery*

At three o'clock on the afternoon they arrived, the two young Gothamites stood with good Brother Cristofer in the great, cold hallway of the monastery to watch the monks march past on their way to the refectory. They came slowly, *pacing* by twos, with their heads bowed, *treading* noiselessly with sandaled feet upon the rough stone flags. As the procession slowly filed past, Eyres suddenly gripped Gilliam by the arm. "Look," he whispered, eagerly, "at the one just opposite you now - the one on this side, with his hand at his waist - if that isn't Johnny Bellchambers then I never saw him!"

Gilliam saw and *recognized* the lost glass of fashion.

"What the *deuce*," said he, wonderingly, "is old Bell doing here? Tommy, it surely can't be he! Never heard of Bell having a turn for the religious. Fact is, I've heard him say things when a four-in-hand didn't seem to tie up just right that would bring him up for *court-martial* before any church."

"It's Bell, without a doubt," said Eyres, firmly, "or I'm pretty badly in need of an oculist. But think of Johnny Bellchambers, the Royal High Chancellor of swell togs and the Mahatma of pink teas, up here in cold storage doing penance in a snuff-coloured bathrobe! I can't get it straight in my mind. Let's ask the jolly old boy that's doing honours."

Brother Cristofer was appealed to for information. By that time the monks had passed into the refectory. He could not tell to which one they referred. Bellchambers? Ah, the brothers of St. Gondrau abandoned their worldly names when they took the vows. Did the gentlemen wish to speak with one of the brothers? If they would come to the refectory and indicate the one they wished to see, the reverend abbot in authority would, doubtless, permit it.

Eyres and Gilliam went into the dining hall and pointed out to Brother Cristofer the man they had seen. Yes, it was Johnny Bellchambers. They saw his face plainly now, as he sat among the *dingy* brothers, never looking up, eating broth from a coarse, brown bowl. Permission to speak to one of the brothers was granted to the two travellers by the *abbot*, and

Rapturous - *Experiencing great joy/delight*
Ineffable - *In capable of being, described in words*
Dingy - *Shabby*
Deuce - *A cost or point of two*
Abbot - *The superior of an abbey of monks*

Greatest Humour Stories

they waited in a reception room for him to come. When he did come, treading softly in his sandals, both Eyres and Gilliam looked at him in perplexity and astonishment. It was Johnny Bellchambers, but he had a different look.

Upon his smooth-shaven face was an expression of ***ineffable*** peace, of ***rapturous*** attainment, of perfect and complete happiness. His form was proudly erect, his eyes shone with a ***serene*** and gracious light. He was as neat and well-groomed as in the old New York days, but how differently was he clad! Now he seemed clothed in but a single garment - a long robe of rough brown cloth, gathered by a cord at the waist, and falling in straight, loose folds nearly to his feet. He shook hands with his visitors with his old ease and grace of manner. If there was any embarrassment in that meeting it was not manifested by Johnny Bellchambers. The room had no seats; they stood to converse.

"Glad to see you, old man," said Eyres, somewhat awkwardly. "Wasn't expecting to find you up here. Not a bad idea though, after all. Society's an awful sham. Must be a relief to shake the giddy whirl and retire to - er - ***contemplation*** and - er - prayer and hymns, and those things."

"Oh, cut that, Tommy," said Bellchambers, cheerfully. "Don't be afraid that I'll pass around the plate. I go through these thing-um-bobs with the rest of these old boys because they are the rules. I'm Brother Ambrose here, you know. I'm given just ten minutes to talk to you fellows. That's rather a new design in waistcoats you have on, isn't it, Gilliam? Are they wearing those things on Broadway now?"

"It's the same old Johnny," said Gilliam, joyfully. "What the devil - I mean why - Oh, confound it! what did you do it for, old man?"

"Peel the bathrobe," pleaded Eyres, almost tearfully, "and go back with us. The old crowd'll go wild to see you. This isn't in your line, Bell. I know half a dozen girls that wore the willow on the quiet when you shook us in that unaccountable

Contemplation -
Deep consideration, reflection, intention
Dispensation -
Distribution
Caressinghy - *An act/gresture expressing offection*
Reverberated -
Rebounded, recoiled

Greatest   Humour   Stories

way. Hand in your resignation, or get a **dispensation**, or whatever you have to do to get a release from this ice factory. You'll get catarrh here, Johnny - and - My God! you haven't any socks on!"

Bellchambers looked down at his sandaled feet and smiled.

"You fellows don't understand," he said, **soothingly**. "It's nice of you to want me to go back, but the old life will never know me again. I have reached here the goal of all my ambitions.

I am entirely happy and contented. Here I shall remain for the remainder of my days. You see this robe that I wear?" Bellchambers **caressingly** touched the straight-hanging garment: "At last I have found something that will not bag at the knees. I have attained -"

At that moment the deep boom of the great brass bell **reverberated** through the monastery. It must have been a **summons** to immediate devotions, for Brother Ambrose bowed his head, turned and left the chamber without another word. A slight wave of his hand as he passed through the stone doorway seemed to say a farewell to his old friends. They left the monastery without seeing him again.

And this is the story that Tommy Eyres and Lancelot Gilliam brought back with them from their latest European tour.

Mirth - *Amusement, laughter*
Partaken - *Receive, take or have a part*
Resentment - *The feeling of displeasure*
Smoldered - *To burn without flame*
Friendly - *Agreeable*

Food For Thought

What do you think Johnny Bellchambers was doing in the monastery? Why did he become a monk and said to his friends, "You see this robe that I wear?" At last, I have found something that will not bag at the knees. I have reached here – the goal of all my ambitions." Think deeply, before giving an appropriate answer.

An Understanding

Q. 1. What was the mystery behind the sudden and unexplained disappearance of Johnny Bellchambers?
Ans. _____
_____
_____
_____
_____

Q. 2. What was the background of Johnny and how was his lifestyle?
Ans. _____
_____
_____
_____
_____

Q. 3. Johnny Bellchambers disappeared and for three days, it was of no concern to his friends. Then everyone was worried as he had no enemies, no debts and no woman. Then what was the actual cause of his disappearance?
Ans. _____
_____
_____
_____
_____

Q. 4. What did Tom Eyres and Lancelot Gilliam, two of Bellchambers' old friends hear and find in a monastery?
Ans. _____
_____
_____
_____
_____

Bertie's Christmas Eve
~ Saki

IT 'was Christmas Eve, and the family circle of Luke Steffink, Esq., was aglow with the amiability and random **mirth** which the occasion demanded. A long and lavish dinner had been **partaken** of, waits had been round and sung carols; the house-party had regaled itself with more **caroling** on its own account, and there had been romping which, even in a pulpit reference, could not have been condemned as **ragging**. In the midst of the general glow, however, there was one black unkindled cinder.

Bertie Steffink, nephew of the **aforementioned** Luke, had early in life adopted the profession of ne'er-do-weel; his father had been something of the kind before him. At the age of eighteen Bertie had commenced that round of visits to our Colonial possessions, so seemly and desirable in the case of a Prince of the Blood, so suggestive of insincerity in a young man of the middle-class. He had gone to grow tea in Ceylon and fruit in British Columbia, and to help sheep to grow wool in Australia. At the age of twenty he had just returned from some similar errand in Canada, from which it may be gathered that the trial he gave to these various experiments was of the summary drum-head nature. Luke Steffink, who fulfilled the troubled role of guardian and deputy-parent to Bertie, deplored the persistent manifestation of the homing instinct on his nephew's part, and his solemn thanks earlier in the day for the blessing of reporting a united family had no reference to Bertie's return.

Arrangements had been promptly made for packing the youth off to a distant corner of Rhodesia, whence return would be a difficult matter; the journey to this uninviting destination was imminent, in fact a more careful and willing traveller would have already begun to think about his packing. Hence Bertie was in no mood to share in the festive spirit which displayed itself around him, and **resentment smouldered** within him at the eager, self-absorbed discussion of social plans for the coming months which he heard on all sides. Beyond depressing his uncle and the family circle generally by singing "Say au revoir, and not good-bye," he had taken no part in the evening's **conviviality**.

Aforementioned - *Mentioned before*
Resentment - M
Caroling - *Singing a christmas song/hymn*
Ragging - *Teasing*

Eleven o'clock had struck some half-hour ago, and the elder Steffinks began to throw out suggestions leading up to that process which they called retiring for the night.

"Come, Teddie, it's time you were in your little bed, you know," said Luke Steffink to his thirteen-year-old son.

"That's where we all ought to be," said Mrs. Steffink.

"There wouldn't be room," said Bertie.

The remark was considered to border on the scandalous; everybody ate *raisins* and almonds with the nervous industry of sheep feeding during threatening weather.

"In Russia," said Horace Bordenby, who was staying in the house as a Christmas guest, "I've read that the peasants believe that if you go into a cow-house or stable at midnight on Christmas Eve you will hear the animals talk. They're supposed to have the gift of speech at that one moment of the year."

"Oh, DO let's ALL go down to the cow-house and listen to what they've got to say!" exclaimed Beryl, to whom anything was thrilling and amusing if you did it in a troop.

Mrs. Steffink made a laughing protest, but gave a virtual consent by saying, "We must all wrap up well, then." The idea seemed a *scatterbrained* one to her, and almost heathenish, but if afforded an opportunity for "throwing the young people together," and as such she welcomed it. Mr. Horace Bordenby was a young man with quite *substantial* prospects, and he had danced with Beryl at a local *subscription* ball a sufficient number of times to warrant the authorised inquiry on the part of the neighbours whether "there was anything in it." Though Mrs. Steffink would not have put it in so many words, she shared the idea of the Russian peasantry that on this night the beast might speak.

The cow-house stood at the junction of the garden with a small *paddock*, an isolated survival, in a suburban neighbourhood; of what had once been a small farm. Luke Steffink was *complacently* proud of his cow-house and his two cows; he felt that they gave him a stamp of solidity which no number of Wyandottes or Orpingtons could impart. They even seemed to link him in a sort of *inconsequent* way with those *patriarchs* who derived importance from their floating capital of flocks and herbs, he-asses and she-asses. It had been an anxious and *momentous* occasion when he had had to decide definitely

Raisins - *Dried grapes*
Substantial - *Enough*
Paddock - *A small usually enclosed field near a stable/barn*
Complacently - *Pleasantly*

between "the Byre" and "the Ranch" for the naming of his villa residence. A December midnight was hardly the moment he would have chosen for showing his farm-building to visitors, but since it was a fine night, and the young people were anxious for an excuse for a mild *frolic*, Luke consented to chaperon the *expedition*. The servants had long since gone to bed, so the house was left in charge of Bertie, who **scornfully** declined to stir out on the pretext of listening to *bovine* conversation.

"We must go quietly," said Luke, as he headed the *procession* of *giggling* young folk, brought up in the rear by the shawled and *hooded* figure of Mrs. Steffink; "I've always laid stress on keeping this a quiet and orderly neighbourhood."

It was a few minutes to midnight when the party reached the cow-house and made its way in by the light of Luke's stable lantern. For a moment every one stood in silence, almost with a feeling of being in church.

"Daisy -- the one lying down -- is by a shorthorn bull out of a Guernsey cow," announced Luke in a hushed voice, which was in keeping with the *foregoing* impression.

"Is she?" said Bordenby, rather as if he had expected her to be by Rembrandt.

"Myrtle is --"

Myrtle's family history was cut short by a little scream from the women of the party.

The cow-house door had closed noiselessly behind them and the key had turned *gratingly* in the lock; then they heard Bertie's voice pleasantly wishing them good-night and his footsteps retreating along the garden path.

Luke Steffink strode to the window; it was a small square opening of the old-fashioned sort, with iron bars let into the stonework.

"Unlock the door this instant," he shouted, with as much air of menacing authority as a hen might assume when screaming through the bars of a coop at a *marauding* hawk. In reply to his summons the hall-door closed with a *defiant* bang.

A neighbouring clock struck the hour of midnight. If the cows had received the gift of human speech at that moment they would not have been able to make themselves heard. Seven or eight other voices were engaged in describing Bertie's present conduct and his general character at a high pressure of excitement and *indignation*.

Frolic - *Merriment, fun, prank*
Expedition - *An excursion*
Scornfuly - *Contemptuously*
Bovine - *Stolid, dull*
Cession - *Surrender*

In the course of half an hour or so everything that it was permissible to say about Bertie had been said some dozens of times, and other topics began to come to the front -- the extreme *mustiness* of the cow-house, the possibility of it catching fire, and the probability of it being a Rowton House for the vagrant rats of the neighbourhood. And still no sign of deliverance came to the unwilling *vigil-keepers*.

Towards one o'clock the sound of rather boisterous and undisciplined carol-singing approached rapidly, and came to a sudden *anchorage*, apparently just outside the garden-gate. A motor-load of youthful "bloods," in a high state of conviviality, had made a temporary halt for repairs; the stoppage, however, did not extend to the vocal efforts of the party, and the watchers in the cow-shed were treated to a highly unauthorised rendering of "Good King Wenceslas," in which the adjective "good" appeared to be very carelessly applied.

The noise had the effect of bringing Bertie out into the garden, but he utterly ignored the pale, angry faces peering out at the cow-house window, and concentrated his attention on the *revellers* outside the gate.

"Wassail, you chaps!" he shouted.

"Wassail, old sport!" they shouted back; "we'd jolly well drink y'r health, only we've nothing to drink it in."

"Come and *wassail* inside," said Bertie *hospitably*; "I'm all alone, and there's heap's of 'wet'."

They were total strangers, but his touch of kindness made them instantly his kin. In another moment the unauthorised version of King Wenceslas, which, like many other scandals, grew worse on repetition, went echoing up the garden path; two of the revellers gave an *impromptu* performance on the way by executing the staircase waltz up the terraces of what Luke Steffink, hitherto with some justification, called his rock-garden. The rock part of it was still there when the waltz had been accorded its third encore. Luke, more than ever like a cooped hen behind the cow-house bars, was in a position to realise the feelings of concert-goers unable to *countermand* the call for an encore which they neither desire or deserve.

The hall door closed with a bang on Bertie's guests, and the sounds of merriment became faint and *muffled* to the weary watchers at the other end of the garden. Presently two *ominous* pops, in quick succession, made themselves distinctly heard.

Mustiness - *Out of date*
Anchorage - *A charge for occupying such an area*
Wassail - *An alcholic drink*
Ominous - *Foreboding evil*
Impromptu - *Made/done without preparation*

"They've got at the champagne!" exclaimed Mrs. Steffink.

"Perhaps it's the sparkling Moselle," said Luke hopefully.

Three or four more pops were heard.

"The *champagne* and the sparkling *Moselle*," said Mrs. Steffink.

Luke uncorked an expletive which, like brandy in a temperance household, was only used on rare emergencies. Mr. Horace Bordenby had been making use of similar expressions under his breath for a considerable time past. The experiment of "throwing the young people together" had been prolonged beyond a point when it was likely to produce any romantic result.

Some forty minutes later the hall door opened and disgorged a crowd that had thrown off any restraint of shyness that might have influenced its earlier actions. Its vocal efforts in the direction of carol singing were now **supplemented** by instrumental music; a Christmas-tree that had been prepared for the children of the gardener and other household retainers had yielded a rich spoil of tin trumpets, rattles, and drums. The life-story of King Wenceslas had been dropped, Luke was thankful to notice, but it was intensely irritating for the chilled prisoners in the cow-house to be told that it was a hot time in the old town tonight, together with some accurate but entirely superfluous information as to the imminence of Christmas morning. Judging by the protests which began to be shouted from the upper windows of neighbouring houses the sentiments prevailing in the cow-house were heartily echoed in other quarters.

The revellers found their car, and, what was more remarkable, managed to drive off in it, with a parting fanfare of tin trumpets. The lively beat of a drum disclosed the fact that the master of the revels remained on the scene.

"Bertie!" came in an angry, *imploring* chorus of shouts and screams from the cow-house window.

"Hullo," cried the owner of the name, turning his rather *errant* steps in the direction of the summons; "are you people still there? Must have heard everything cows got to say by this time. If you haven't, no use waiting. After all, it's a Russian legend, and *Russian Chrismush Eve* not due for 'nother fortnight. Better come out."

Champagne - *The speaking dry, white table*
Moselle - *A light, white wine of Germany*
Supplemented - *Added*
Imploring - *To beg earnestly*
Errant - *Moving aimlessly*

Ineffectual - *Inefficient, inept*
Lusty - *Greedy*
Accompaniment - *Complement, supplement*
Exuberant - *Full of enregy, cheerful*
Rotten - *Decayed*

After one or two ineffectual attempts he managed to pitch the key of the cow-house door in through the window. Then, lifting his voice in the strains of "I'm afraid to go home in the dark," with a lusty drum accompaniment, he led the way back to the house. The hurried procession of the released that followed in his steps came in for a good deal of the adverse comment that his exuberant display had evoked.

It was the happiest Christmas Eve he had ever spent. To quote his own words, he had a rotten Christmas.

Food For Thought

How did Bertie enjoy his Christmas eve? How did the revellers join him and what did Bertie and the revellers do while the elders were away in the cow-house waiting anxiously for the animals to talk after midnight? Do you believe that such things do happen even in this modern age?

An Understanding

Q. 1. How did Luke Steffink's family celebrate their Christmas? Who was Bertie Steffink, how old was he and what were his experiences in life?
Ans. _____
_____
_____
_____
_____

Q. 2. Why was Bertie depressed and in no mood to share in the festive spirit which displayed itself around him?
Ans. _____
_____
_____
_____
_____

Q. 3. Who was Horace Bordenby and what did he read about a cow-house or a stable on Christmas eve?
Ans. _____
_____
_____
_____
_____

Q. 4. Where was the cow-house located in the Steffink household? What happened there at midnight on the Christmas eve day? Who led the procession of the giggling and amused young folk who were present at the Steffink household on the Christmas eve?
Ans. _____
_____
_____
_____
_____

Proof Of The Pudding
~ O. Henry

SPring winked a vitreous optic at Editor Westbrook of the *Minerva Magazine*, and deflected him from his course. He had lunched in his favorite corner of a Broadway hotel, and was returning to his office when his feet became entangled in the lure of the vernal **coquette**. Which is by way of saying that he turned eastward in Twenty-sixth Street, safely forded the spring freshet of vehicles in Fifth Avenue, and meandered along the walks of budding Madison Square.

The lenient air and the settings of the little park almost formed a pastoral; the color ***motif*** was green - the presiding shade at the creation of man and vegetation.

The callow grass between the walks was the colour of verdigris, a poisonous green, ***reminiscent*** of the horde of derelict humans that had breathed upon the soil during the summer and autumn. The bursting tree buds looked strangely familiar to those who had botanised among the ***garnishings*** of the fish course of a forty-cent dinner. The sky above was of that pale aquamarine tint that ballroom poets rhyme with "true" and "Sue" and "coo." The one natural and frank color visible was the ostensible green of the newly painted benches - a shade between the color of a pickled cucumber and that of a last year's fast-black ***cravenette*** raincoat. But, to the city-bred eye of Editor Westbrook, the landscape appeared a masterpiece.

And now, whether you are of those who rush in, or of the gentle ***concourse*** that fears to tread, you must follow in a brief invasion of the editor's mind.

Editor Westbrook's spirit was contented and serene. The April number of the *Minerva* had sold its entire edition before the tenth day of the month - a newsdealer in Keokuk had written that he could have sold fifty copies more if he had 'em. The owners of the magazine had raised his (the editor's) salary; he had just installed in his home a jewel of a recently imported cook who was afraid of policemen; and the morning papers had published in full a speech he had made at a publishers' banquet. Also there were echoing in his mind the jubilant notes of a splendid song that his charming young wife had sung to him before he left his up-town apartment that morning. She

Coquette - *A woman who flirts lighthearted with man*
Motif - *A dominant idea feature*
Reminiscent - *Stimulating memories*
Cravenetle - *Timidly*
Concourse - *Assemblase*

was taking *enthusiastic* interest in her music of late, practising early and diligently. When he had complimented her on the improvement in her voice she had fairly hugged him for joy at his praise. He felt, too, the benign, tonic medicament of the trained nurse, Spring, tripping softly adown the wards of the *convalescent* city.

While Editor Westbrook was sauntering between the rows of park benches (already filling with vagrants and the guardians of lawless childhood) he felt his sleeve grasped and held. Suspecting that he was about to be *panhandled*, he turned a cold and unprofitable face, and saw that his captor was - Dawe - Shackleford Dawe, dingy, almost ragged, the *genteel* scracely visible in him through the deeper lines of the shabby.

While the editor is pulling himself out of his surprise, a flashlight biography of Dawe is offered.

He was a fiction writer, and one of Westbrook's old acquaintances. At one time they might have called each other old friends. Dawe had some money in those days, and lived in a decent apartment house near Westbrook's. The two families often went to theatres and dinners together. Mrs. Dawe and Mrs. Westbrook became "dearest" friends. Then one day a little tentacle of the octopus, just to amuse itself, ingurgitated Dawe's capital, and he moved to the Gramercy Park neighborhood where one, for a few groats per week, may sit upon one's trunk under eight-branched chandeliers and opposite Carrara marble **mantels** and watch the mice play upon the floor. Dawe thought to live by writing fiction. Now and then he sold a story. He submitted many to Westbrook.

The *Minerva* printed one or two of them; the rest were returned. Westbrook sent a careful and conscientious personal letter with each rejected manuscript, pointing out in detail his reasons for considering it unavailable. Editor Westbrook had his own clear conception of what constituted good fiction. So had Dawe. Mrs. Dawe was mainly concerned about the constituents of the scanty dishes of food that she managed to scrape together.

One day Dawe had been spouting to her about the *excellencies* of certain French writers. At dinner they sat down to a dish that a hungry schoolboy could have *encompassed* at a gulp. Dawe commented.

Convalescent - *Gradual return to health after illness*
Genteelc - *Well-bred, refined*
Mantels - *Wooden/stone frame around the opening of a fireplace*

"It's Maupassant hash," said Mrs. Dawe. "It may not be art, but I do wish you would do a five-course Marion Crawford serial with an Ella Wheeler Wilcox **sonnet** for dessert. I'm hungry."

As far as this from success was Shackleford Dawe when he plucked Editor Westbrook's sleeve in Madison Square. That was the first time the editor had seen Dawe in several months.

"Why, Shack, is this you?" said Westbrook, somewhat awkwardly, for the form of his phrase seemed to touch upon the other's changed appearance.

"Sit down for a minute," said Dawe, **tugging** at his sleeve. "This is my office. I can't come to yours, looking as I do. Oh, sit down - you won't be disgraced. Those half-plucked birds on the other benches will take you for a swell porch-climber. They won't know you are only an editor."

"Smoke, Shack?" said Editor Westbrook, sinking cautiously upon the **virulent** green bench. He always yielded gracefully when he did yield.

Dawe snapped at the cigar as a kingfisher darts at a sunperch, or a girl pecks at a chocolate cream.

"I have just -" began the editor.

"Oh, I know; don't finish," said Dawe. "Give me a match. You have just ten minutes to spare. How did you manage to get past my office-boy and invade my sanctum? There he goes now, throwing his club at a dog that couldn't read the 'Keep off the Grass' signs."

"How goes the writing?" asked the editor.

"Look at me," said Dawe, "for your answer. Now don't put on that embarrassed, friendly-but-honest look and ask me why I don't get a job as a wine agent or a cab driver. I'm in the fight to a finish. I know I can write good fiction and I'll force you fellows to admit it yet. I'll make you change the spelling of 'regrets' to 'c-h-e-q-u-e' before I'm done with you."

Editor Westbrook gazed through his nose-glasses with a sweetly sorrowful, omniscient, sympathetic, skeptical expression - the copyrighted expression of the editor **beleagured** by the unavailable contributor.

"Have you read the last story I sent you - 'The Alarum of the Soul'?" asked Dawe.

Sonnet - *A poem of 14 lines*
Tugging - *To pull at*
Virulent - *Actively, poisonous*
Beleagred - *With forces*

"Carefully. I hesitated over that story, Shack, really I did. It had some good points. I was writing you a letter to send with it when it goes back to you. I regret -"

"Never mind the regrets," said Dawe, grimly. "There's neither salve nor sting in 'em any more. What I want to know is *why*. Come now; out with the good points first."

"The story," said Westbrook, **deliberately**, after a suppressed sigh, "is written around an almost original plot. Characterisation - the best you have done. Construction - almost as good, except for a few weak joints which might be strengthened by a few changes and touches. It was a good story, except -"

"I can write English, can't I?" interrupted Dawe.

"I have always told you," said the editor, "that you had a style."

"Then the trouble is -"

"Same old thing," said Editor Westbrook. "You work up to your climax like an artist. And then you turn yourself into a photographer. I don't know what form of obstinate madness possesses you, but that is what you do with everything that you write.

No, I will retract the comparison with the photographer. Now and then photography, in spite of its impossible perspective, manages to record a fleeting glimpse of truth. But you spoil every **denouement** by those flat, drab, obliterating strokes of your brush that I have so often complained of. If you would rise to the literary pinnacle of your dramatic senses, and paint them in the high colors that art requires, the postman would leave fewer bulky, self-addressed envelopes at your door."

"Oh, **fiddles** and footlights!" cried Dawe, derisively. "You've got that old sawmill drama kink in your brain yet. When the man with the black mustache kidnaps golden-haired Bessie you are bound to have the mother kneel and raise her hands in the spotlight and say: 'May high heaven witness that I will rest neither night nor day till the heartless villain that has stolen me child feels the weight of another's vengeance!'"

Editor Westbrook conceded a smile of **impervious complacency**.

Deliberately - *Intentional*
Denouement - *The final resolution*
Riddles - *Puzzles*
Impervious - *Impenetrable*
Complacency - *Friendly, guilty*

"I think," said he, "that in real life the woman would express herself in those words or in very similar ones."

"Not in a six hundred nights' run anywhere but on the stage," said Dawe hotly. "I'll tell you what she'd say in real life. She'd say: 'What! Bessie led away by a strange man? Good Lord! It's one trouble after another! Get my other hat, I must hurry around to the police-station. Why wasn't somebody looking after her, I'd like to know?

For God's sake, get out of my way or I'll never get ready. Not that hat - the brown one with the velvet bows. Bessie must have been crazy; she's usually shy of strangers. Is that too much powder? Lordy! How I'm upset!'

"That's the way she'd talk," continued Dawe. "People in real life don't fly into heroics and blank verse at emotional crises. They simply can't do it. If they talk at all on such occasions they draw from the same vocabulary that they use every day, and muddle up their words and ideas a little more, that's all."

"Shack," said Editor Westbrook impressively, "did you ever pick up the *mangled* and lifeless form of a child from under the *fender* of a street car, and carry it in your arms and lay it down before the *distracted* mother? Did you ever do that and listen to the words of grief and despair as they flowed spontaneously from her lips?"

"I never did," said Dawe. "Did you?"

"Well, no," said Editor Westbrook, with a slight frown. "But I can well imagine what she would say."

"So can I," said Dawe.

And now the fitting time had come for Editor Westbrook to play the oracle and silence his opinioned contributor. It was not for an unarrived fictionist to dictate words to be uttered by the heroes and heroines of the *Minerva Magazine*, contrary to the theories of the editor thereof.

"My dear Shack," said he, "if I know anything of life I know that every sudden, deep and tragic emotion in the human heart calls forth an apposite, concordant, conformable and proportionate expression of feeling.

How much of this inevitable accord between expression and feeling should be attributed to nature, and how much to the influence of art, it would be difficult to say. The *sublimely* terrible roar of the lioness that has been deprived of her cubs is

Mangled - *Severely, disfigure*
Fender - *A device on the front of a locomotive*
Sublimely - *Completely, absolutely*
Histrionic - *Overly dramatic*

dramatically as far above her customary whine and purr as the kingly and transcendent utterances of Lear are above the level of his senile vaporings. But it is also true that all men and women have what may be called a sub-conscious dramatic sense that is awakened by a sufficiently deep and powerful emotion - a sense unconsciously acquired from literature and the stage that prompts them to express those emotions in language *befitting* their importance and *histrionic* value."

"And in the name of the seven sacred saddle-blankets of Sagittarius, where did the stage and literature get the stunt?" asked Dawe.

"From life," answered the editor, triumphantly.

The story writer rose from the bench and *gesticulated eloquently* but dumbly. He was beggared for words with which to formulate adequately his dissent.

On a bench nearby a frowzy loafer opened his red eyes and *perceived* that his moral support was due a downtrodden brother.

"Punch him one, Jack," he called hoarsely to Dawe. "W'at's he come makin' a noise like a penny arcade for amongst gen'lemen that comes in the square to set and think?"

Editor Westbrook looked at his watch with an affected show of leisure.

"Tell me," asked Dawe, with *truculent* anxiety, "what especial faults in 'The Alarum of the Soul' caused you to throw it down?"

"When Gabriel Murray," said Westbrook, "goes to his telephone and is told that his fiancee has been shot by a burglar, he says - I do not recall the exact words, but -"

"I do," said Dawe. "He says: 'Damn Central; she always cuts me off.' (And then to his friend) 'Say, Tommy, does a thirty-two bullet make a big hole? It's kind of hard luck, ain't it? Could you get me a drink from the sideboard, Tommy? No; straight; nothing on the side.'"

"And again," continued the editor, without pausing for argument, "when Berenice opens the letter from her husband informing her that he has fled with the manicure girl, her words are - let me see -"

"She says," *interposed* the author: "'Well, what do you think of that!'"

Gesticulated - *To express in gestures*
Eloquently - *Fluently*
Truculent - *Firece, cruel*
Colloquialisms - *Informal words*
Doggedly - *Stubbornly*

"Absurdly inappropriate words," said Westbrook, "presenting an anti-climax - plunging the story into hopeless bathos. Worse yet; they mirror life falsely. No human being ever uttered banal **colloquialisms** when **confronted** by sudden tragedy."

"Wrong," said Dawe, closing his unshaven jaws **doggedly**. "I say no man or woman ever spouts 'high-falutin' talk when they go up against a real climax. They talk naturally and a little worse."

The editor rose from the bench with his air of *indulgence* and inside information.

"Say, Westbrook," said Dawe, *pinning* him by the *lapel*, "would you have accepted 'The Alarum of the Soul' if you had believed that the actions and words of the characters were true to life in the parts of the story that we discussed?"

"It is very likely that I would, if I believed that way," said the editor. "But I have explained to you that I do not."

"If I could prove to you that I am right?"

"I'm sorry, Shack, but I'm afraid I haven't time to argue any further just now."

"I don't want to argue," said Dave. "I want to demonstrate to you from life itself that my view is the correct one."

"How could you do that?" asked Westbrook, in a surprised tone.

"Listen," said the writer, seriously. "I have thought of a way. It is important to me that my theory of true-to-life fiction be recognised as correct by the magazines. I've fought for it for three years, and I'm down to my last dollar, with two months' rent due."

"I have applied the opposite of your theory," said the editor, "in selecting the fiction for the *Minerva Magazine*. The circulation has gone up from ninety thousand to -"

"Four hundred thousand," said Dawe. "Whereas it should have been *boosted* to a million."

"You said something to me just now about demonstrating your pet theory."

"I will. If you'll give me about half an hour of your time I'll prove to you that I am right. I'll prove it by Louise."

"Your wife!" exclaimed Westbrook. "How?"

"Well, not exactly by her, but *with* her," said Dawe. "Now, you know how devoted and loving Louse has always been.

Indulgence - *Tolerance*
Pinning -*Longing*
Lapel - *Especially a continuation of at collar*
Boosted - *Lifted/Raised*

She thinks I'm the only genuine preparation on the market that bears the old doctor's signature. She's been fonder and more faithful than ever, since I've been cast for the neglected genius part."

"Indeed, she is a charming and admirable life companion," agreed the editor. "I remember what inseparable friends she and Mrs. Westbrook once were. We are both lucky chaps, Shack, to have such wives. You must bring Mrs. Dawe up some evening soon, and we'll have one of those informal chafing-dish suppers that we used to enjoy so much."

"Later," said Dawe. "When I get another shirt. And now I'll tell you my scheme. When I was about to leave home after breakfast - if you can call tea and oatmeal breakfast - Louise told me she was going to visit her aunt in Eighty-ninth Street. She said she would return at three o'clock. She is always on time to a minute. It is now -"

Dawe glanced toward the editor's watch pocket.

"Twenty-seven minutes to three," said Westbrook, scanning his time-piece.

"We have just enough time," said Dawe. "We will go to my flat at once. I will write a note, address it to her and leave it on the table where she will see it as she enters the door. You and I will be in the dining-room concealed by the *portieres*. In that note I'll say that I have fled from her forever with an affinity who understands the need of my artistic soul as she never did. When she reads it we will observe her actions and hear her words. Then we will know which theory is the correct one - yours or mine."

"Oh, never!" exclaimed the editor, shaking his head. "That would be *inexcusably* cruel. I could not consent to have Mrs. Dawe's feelings played upon in such a manner."

"Brace up," said the writer. "I guess I think as much of her as you do. It's for her benefit as well as mine. I've got to get a market for my stories in some way.

It won't hurt Louise. She's healthy and sound. Her heart goes as strong as a ninety-eight-cent watch. It'll last for only a minute, and then I'll step out and explain to her. You really owe it to me to give me the chance, Westbrook."

Editor Westbrook at length yielded, though but half willingly. And in the half of him that consented lurked the ***vivisectionist*** that is in all of us. Let him who has not used

Portieres - *Curtains hung in a doorway*
Inexcusably - *Incapable of being excused/justified*
Vivisectionist - *A person who dissects the living body*

Greatest Humour Stories

the scalpel rise and stand in his place. Pity 'tis that there are not enough rabbits and guinea-pigs to go around.

The two experimenters in Art left the Square and hurried eastward and then to that south until they arrived in the Gramercy neighbourhood.

Within its high iron railings the little park had put on its smart coat of *vernal* green, and was admiring itself in its fountain mirror. Outside the railings the hollow square of crumbling houses, shells of a *bygone* gentry, leaned as if in ghostly gossip over the forgotten doings of the vanished quality. *Sic transit gloria urbis.*

A block or two north of the Park, Dawe steered the editor again eastward, then, after covering a short distance, into a lofty but narrow flathouse burdened with a *floridly* overdecorated *fa,cade.* To the fifth story they toiled, and Dawe, panting, pushed his latch-key into the door of one of the front flats.

When the door opened Editor Westbrook saw, with feelings of pity, how meanly and *meagerly* the rooms were furnished.

"Get a chair, if you can find one," said Dawe, "while I hunt up pen and ink. Hello, what's this? Here's a note from Louise. She must have left it there when she went out this morning."

He picked up an envelope that lay on the centre-table and tore it open. He began to read the letter that he drew out of it; and once having begun it aloud he so read it through to the end. These are the words that Editor Westbrook heard:

"Dear Shackleford:

"By the time you get this I will be about a hundred miles away and still a-going. I've got a place in the chorus of the Occidental Opera Co., and we start on the road to-day at twelve o'clock. I didn't want to starve to death, and so I decided to make my own living. I'm not coming back. Mrs. Westbrook is going with me.

She said she was tired of living with a combination *phonograph*, iceberg and dictionary, and she's not coming back, either. We've been practising the songs and dances for two months on the quiet. I hope you will be successful, and get along all right! Good-bye.

Floridly - *Reddish, ruddy*
Meagerly - *Hardly*
Phonograph - *A form of gramophone*
Blurted - *Revealed, utter suddenly*

"Louise."

Dawe dropped the letter, covered his face with his trembling hands, and cried out in a deep, vibrating voice:

"*My God, why hast thou given me this cup to drink? Since she is false, then let Thy Heaven's fairest gifts, faith and love, become the jesting by-words of traitors and fiends!*"

Editor Westbrook's glasses fell to the floor. The fingers of one hand *fumbled* with a button on his coat as he *blurted* between his pale lips:

"*Say, Shack, ain't that a hell of a note? Wouldn't that knock you off your perch, Shack? Ain't it hell, now, Shack - ain't it?*"

Food For Thought

O.Henry is known for surprise endings. Dawe was an unsuccessful writer and Westbrook, a struggling editor of a magazine, who had recently got a salary raise. Both their wives, particularly, Dawe's wife, Louise was totally disappointed by her husband's unsuccessful career. Do you like the ending of the stroy? Answer in Yes, or No and give reasons for your answer.

An Understanding

Q. 1. Who was Westbrook and how did he increase the sale and circulation of his magazine, *Minerva*?
Ans. _____
_____
_____
_____
_____

Q. 2. The author, O. Henry is known to have a love for nature and uses symbolic language related to nature to depict the various moods of the situations and characters in almost all his short stories. How does he use the same skill in this story?
Ans. _____
_____
_____
_____
_____

Q. 3. When Editor Westbrook was sauntering between the rows of the park benches, he felt his sleeve grasped and held. Who held his hand and how did Westbrook know him?
Ans. _____
_____
_____
_____
_____

Q. 4. How did Louise, Dawe's wife surprised Dawe and Editor Westbrook? Why did Mrs. Westbrook too accompanied Louise and why did both of them leave their husbands?
Ans. _____
_____
_____
_____
_____

Esme

~ Saki

"All hunting stories are the same," said Clovis; "just as all Turf stories are the same, and all--"

"My hunting story isn't a bit like any you've ever heard," said the Baroness. "It happened quite a while ago, when I was about twenty-three. I wasn't living apart from my husband then; you see, neither of us could afford to make the other a separate allowance. In spite of everything that proverbs may say, poverty keeps together more homes than it breaks up. But we always hunted with different packs. All this has nothing to do with the story."

"We haven't arrived at the meet yet. I suppose there was a meet," said Clovis.

"Of course there was a meet," said the Baroness; "all the usual crowd were there, especially Constance Broddle. Constance is one of those **strapping** florid girls that go so well with autumn scenery or Christmas decorations in church. 'I feel a **presentiment** that something dreadful is going to happen,' she said to me; 'am I looking pale?'

"She was looking about as pale as a beetroot that has suddenly heard bad news.

" 'You're looking nicer than usual,' I said, 'but that's so easy for you.' Before she had got the right bearings of this remark we had settled down to business; hounds had found a fox lying out in some gorse-bushes."

"I knew it," said Clovis; "in every fox-hunting story that I've ever heard there's been a fox and some gorse-bushes."

"Constance and I were well mounted," continued the Baroness serenely, "and we had no difficulty in keeping ourselves in the first flight, though it was a fairly stiff run. Towards the finish, however, we must have held rather too independent a line, for we lost the hounds, and found ourselves *plodding* aimlessly along miles away from anywhere. It was fairly *exasperating*, and my temper was beginning to let itself

Strapping - *Powerfully built*
Presentiment - *Foreboding*
Plodding - *To walk heavily*
Exasperating - *To irritate, provoke*

go by inches, when on pushing our way through an accommodating hedge we were gladdened by the sight of hounds in full cry in a hollow just beneath us.

" 'There they go,' cried Constance, and then added in a gasp, 'In Heaven's name, what are they hunting?'

"It was certainly no mortal fox. It stood more than twice as high, had a short, ugly head, and an enormous thick neck.

" 'It's a hyena,' I cried; 'it must have escaped from Lord Pabham's Park.'

"At that moment the hunted beast turned and faced its **pursuers**, and the **hounds** (there were only about six couple of them) stood round in a half-circle and looked foolish. Evidently, they had broken away from the rest of the pack on the trail of this alien scent, and were not quite sure how to treat their **quarry** now they had got him.

"The hyena hailed our approach with unmistakable relief and demonstrations of friendliness. It had probably been accustomed to uniform kindness from humans, while its first experience of a pack of hounds had left a bad impression. The hounds looked more than ever embarrassed as their quarry paraded its sudden intimacy with us, and the faint toot of a horn in the distance was seized on as a welcome signal for **unobtrusive** departure. Constance and I and the hyena were left alone in the gathering twilight.

" 'What are we to do?' asked Constance.

" 'What a person you are for questions,' I said.

" 'Well, we can't stay here all night with a hyena,' she retorted.

" 'I don't know what your ideas of comfort are,' I said; 'but I shouldn't think of staying here all night even without a hyena. My home may be an unhappy one, but at least it has hot and cold water laid on, and domestic service, and other conveniences which we shouldn't find here. We had better make for that ridge of trees to the right; I imagine the Crowley road is just beyond.'

"We **trotted** off slowly along a faintly marked cart-track, with the beast following cheerfully at our heels.

" 'What on earth are we to do with the hyena?' came the *inevitable* question.

Pursuers - *A person who is trying to overtake*
Hounds - *Wild dogs*
Quarry - *An excavation*
Unobtrusiv - *In conspicuous, unassertive*
Trotted - *To walk fast*
Inevitabl - *Destined*

" 'What does one generally do with hyenas?' I asked crossly.

" 'I've never had anything to do with one before,' said Constance.

" 'Well, neither have I. If we even knew its sex we might give it a name. Perhaps we might call it Esme. That would do in either case.

"There was still sufficient daylight for us to distinguish wayside objects, and our listless spirits gave an upward perk as we came upon a small half-naked gipsy brat picking blackberries from a low-growing bush.

The sudden *apparition* of two horsewomen and a hyena set it off crying, and in any case we should scarcely have gleaned any useful geographical information from that source; but there was a probability that we might strike a gipsy *encampment* somewhere along our route. We rode on hopefully but uneventfully for another mile or so.

" 'I wonder what the child was doing there,' said Constance presently.

" 'Picking blackberries. Obviously.'

" 'I don't like the way it cried,' pursued Constance; 'somehow its wail keeps ringing in my ears.'

"I did not chide Constance for her morbid fancies; as a matter of fact the same sensation, of being pursued by a ***persistent fretful wail***, had been forcing itself on my rather over-tired nerves. For company's sake I hulloed to Esme, who had lagged somewhat behind. With a few springy bounds he drew up level, and then shot past us.

"The wailing accompaniment was explained. The gipsy child was firmly, and I expect painfully, held in his jaws.

" 'Merciful Heaven!' screamed Constance, 'what on earth shall we do? What are we to do?'

"I am perfectly certain that at the Last Judgment Constance will ask more questions than any of the examining Seraphs.

" 'Can't we do something?' she persisted tearfully, as Esme cantered easily along in front of our tired horses.

"Personally I was doing everything that occurred to me at the moment. I stormed and scolded and ***coaxed*** in English and

Apparition - *A supernatural appearance of a person*
Encampment - *The act of setting up a camp*
Persistent - *Lasting*
Coaxed - *To influence*
Lumbered - *To put timber*

French and gamekeeper language; I made absurd, ineffectual cuts in the air with my thongless hunting-crop; I hurled my sandwich case at the brute; in fact, I really don't know what more I could have done. And still we **lumbered** on through the deepening dusk, with that dark uncouth shape lumbering ahead of us, and a drone of lugubrious music floating in our ears.

Suddenly Esme bounded aside into some thick bushes, where we could not follow; the wail rose to a **shriek** and then stopped altogether. This part of the story I always hurry over, because it is really rather horrible. When the beast joined us again, after an absence of a few minutes, there was an air of patient understanding about him, as though he knew that he had done something of which we disapproved, but which he felt to be thoroughly justifiable.

" 'How can you let that *ravening* beast trot by your side?' asked Constance. She was looking more than ever like an albino beetroot.

" 'In the first place, I can't prevent it,' I said; 'and in the second place, whatever else he may be, I doubt if he's ravening at the present moment.'

"Constance **shuddered**. 'Do you think the poor little thing suffered much?' came another of her futile questions.

" 'The indications were all that way,' I said; 'on the other hand, of course, it may have been crying from sheer temper. Children sometimes do.'

"It was nearly pitch-dark when we emerged suddenly into the high road. A flash of lights and the whir of a motor went past us at the same moment at uncomfortably close quarters. A thud and a sharp screeching yell followed a second later. The car drew up, and when I had ridden back to the spot I found a young man bending over a dark motionless mass lying by the roadside.

" 'You have killed my Esme,' I exclaimed bitterly.

" 'I'm so awfully sorry,' said the young man; 'I keep dogs myself, so I know what you must feel about it. I'll do anything I can in reparation.'

Shriek - *Loud noised*
Ravening - *Voracious*
Interments - *Firmly resolved*
Contingencies - *Facts/ events*
Resolutely - *The act/ ceremony of burial*

" 'Please bury him at once,' I said; 'that much I think I may ask of you.

" 'Bring the spade, William,' he called to the chauffeur. Evidently hasty roadside *interments* were *contingencies* that had been provided against.

"The digging of a sufficiently large grave took some little time. 'I say, what a magnificent fellow,' said the motorist as the corpse was rolled over into the trench. 'I'm afraid he must have been rather a valuable animal.'

" 'He took second in the puppy class at Birmingham last year,' I said *resolutely*.

Constance *snorted* loudly.

"'Don't cry, dear,' I said brokenly; 'it was all over in a moment. He couldn't have suffered much.'

"'Look here,' said the young fellow *desperately*, 'you simply must let me do something by way of reparation.'

"I refused sweetly, but as he persisted I let him have my address.

"Of course, we kept our own counsel as to the earlier episodes of the evening. Lord Pabham never advertised the loss of his hyena; when a strictly fruit-eating animal strayed from his park a year or two previously he was called upon to give compensation in eleven cases of sheep-worrying and practically to re-stock his neighbours' poultry-yards, and an escaped hyena would have mounted up to something on the scale of a Government grant. The gipsies were equally *unobtrusive* over their missing offspring; I don't suppose in large *encampments* they really know to a child or two how many they've got."

The Baroness paused *reflectively*, and then continued:

"There was a *sequel* to the adventure, though. I got through the post a charming little diamond broach, with the name Esme set in a sprig of rosemary. Incidentally, too, I lost the friendship of Constance Broddle. You see, when I sold the brooch I quite properly refused to give her any share of the proceeds. I pointed

Snorted - *Breathe violently*
Desperately - *In urgent need*
Unobtrusive - *Inconspicuous*
Encampments - *Setting up camps*
Sequel - *A literary work, movie, etc.*

out that the Esme part of the affair was my own invention, and the hyena part of it belonged to Lord Pabham, if it really was his hyena, of which, of course, I've no proof."

Food For Thought

Why do you think the Baroness lost her friendship with Constance Broddle? Do you think that almost all stories of Saki have a deeper meaning or a hidden element in them? If Yes, you find out the message that has been reflected from this story? Give your answer in five to six lines.

An Understanding

Q. 1. What is the story all about? How was the hunting story of the Baroness different from the usual Turf stories? To whom was the Baroness telling the story?
Ans. _____
_____
_____
_____
_____

Q. 2. Who was Constance Broddle? Where did she accompany the Baroness and what happened during their hunting expedition?
Ans. _____
_____
_____
_____
_____

Q. 3. Where did the Hyena escape from? The Baroness immediately took the baby Hyena but Constance was not sure as to what they would do with it. What did they finally do with the hyena?
Ans. _____
_____
_____
_____
_____

Q. 4. Who was 'Esme'? Why did the Baroness added the 'Esme' Part in her story as her own invention?
Ans. _____
_____
_____
_____
_____

Babes In The Jungle
~ O. Henry

MOntague Silver, the finest street man and art grafter in the West, says to me once in Little Rock: "If you ever lose your mind, Billy, and get too old to do honest **swindling** among grown men, go to New York. In the West a sucker is born every minute; but in New York they appear in chunks of roe - you can't count 'em!"

Two years afterward I found that I couldn't remember the names of the Russian admirals, and I noticed some gray hairs over my left ear; so I knew the time had arrived for me to take Silver's advice.

I struck New York about noon one day, and took a walk up Broadway. And I run against Silver himself, all encompassed up in a spacious kind of haberdashery, leaning against a hotel and rubbing the half-moons on his nails with a silk handkerchief.

"Paresis or **superannuated**?" I asks him.

"Hello, Billy," says Silver; "I'm glad to see you. Yes, it seemed to me that the West was accumulating a little too much wiseness. I've been saving New York for dessert. I know it's a low-down trick to take things from these people. They only know this and that and pass to and fro and think ever and anon. I'd hate for my mother to know I was skinning these weak-minded ones. She raised me better."

"Is there a crush already in the waiting rooms of the old doctor that does skin **grafting**?" I asks.

"Well, no," says Silver; "you needn't back Epidermis to win today. I've only been here a month. But I'm ready to begin; and the members of Willie Manhattan's Sunday School class, each of whom has volunteered to contribute a portion of cuticle toward this **rehabilitation**, may as well send their photos to the *Evening Daily*.

"I've been studying the town," says Silver, "and reading the papers every day, and I know it as well as the cat in the City Hall knows an O'Sullivan. People here lie down on the floor and scream and kick when you are the least bit slow about taking money from them. Come up in my room and I'll tell you. We'll work the town together, Billy, for the sake of old times."

Swindling - *Cheating*
Superannuated - *Retired because of age*
Grafting - *Implanting, transplanting*
Rehabilitation - *Restore to a condition of good health*

Silver takes me up in a hotel. He has a quantity of irrelevant objects lying about.

"There's more ways of getting money from these metropolitan **hayseeds**," says Silver, "than there is of cooking rice in Charleston, S. C. They'll bite at anything. The brains of most of 'em commute. The wiser they are in intelligence the less perception of **cognizance** they have. Why, didin't a man the other day sell J. P. Morgan an oil portrait of Rockefeller, Jr., for Andrea del Sarto's celebrated painting of the young Saint John!

"You see that bundle of printed stuff in the corner, Billy? That's gold mining stock. I started out one day to sell that, but I quit it in two hours. Why? Got arrested for blocking the street. People fought to buy it. I sold the policeman a block of it on the way to the station-house, and then I took it off the market. I don't want people to give me their money. I want some little consideration connected with the transaction to keep my pride from being hurt. I want 'em to guess the missing letter in Chic-go, or draw to a pair of nines before they pay me a cent of money.

"Now there's another little scheme that worked so easy I had to quit it. You see that bottle of blue ink on the table? I tattooed an anchor on the back of my hand and went to a bank and told 'em I was Admiral Dewey's nephew. They offered to cash my draft on him for a thousand, but I didn't know my uncle's first name. It shows, though, what an easy town it is. As for burglars, they won't go in a house now unless there's a hot supper ready and a few college students to wait on 'em. They're slugging citizens all over the upper part of the city and I guess, taking the town from end to end, it's a plain case of **assault** and Battery."

"Monty," says I, when Silver had **slacked**, up, "you may have Manhattan correctly discriminated in your perorative, but I doubt it. I've only been in town two hours, but it don't dawn upon me that it's ours with a cherry in it. There ain't enough rus in urbe about it to suit me. I'd be a good deal much better satisfied if the citizens had a straw or more in their hair, and run more to **velveteen** vests and buckeye watch charms. They don't look easy to me."

"You've got it, Billy," says Silver. "All emigrants have it. New York's bigger than Little Rock or Europe, and it frightens a foreigner. You'll be all right. I tell you I feel like slapping

Hayseeds - *Seeds*
Cognizance - *Awareness*
Assault - *A sudden*
Slacked - *Loosened*
Velveteen - *A cotton fabric resembling velvet*

the people here because they don't send me all their money in laundry baskets, with **germicide** sprinkled over it. I hate to go down on the street to get it. Who wears the diamonds in this town? Why, Winnie, the Wiretapper's wife, and Bella, the Buncosteerer's bride. New Yorkers can be worked easier than a blue rose on a tidy. The only thing that bothers me is I know I'll break the cigars in my vest pocket when I get my clothes all full of twenties."

"I hope you are right, Monty," says I; "but I wish all the same I had been satisfied with a small business in Little Rock. The crop of farmers is never so short out there but what you can get a few of 'em to sign a petition for a new post office that you can discount for $200 at the county bank. The people hear appear to possess **instincts** of **self-preservation** and illiberality. I fear me that we are not cultured enough to tackle this game."

"Don't worry," says Silver. "I've got this Jayville-near-Tarrytown correctly estimated as sure as North River is the Hudson and East River ain't a river. Why, there are people living in four blocks of Broadway who never saw any kind of a building except a *skyscraper* in their lives! A good, live hustling Western man ought to get conspicuous enough here inside of three months to incur either Jerome's **clemency** or Lawson's displeasure."

"Hyperbole aside," says I, "do you know of any immediate system of **buncoing** the community out of a dollar or two except by applying to the Salvation Army or having a fit on Miss Helen Gould's doorsteps?"

"Dozens of 'em," says Silver. "How much capital have you got, Billy?"

"A thousand," I told him.

"I've got $1,200," says he. "We'll pool and do a big piece of business. There's so many ways we can make a million that I don't know how to begin."

The next morning Silver meets me at the hotel and he is all ***sonorous*** and stirred with a kind of silent joy.

"We're to meet J. P. Morgan this afternoon," says he. "A man I know in the hotel wants to introduce us. He's a friend of his. He says he likes to meet people from the West."

"That sounds nice and ***plausible***," says I. "I'd like to know Mr. Morgan."

Germicide -*Any substance that kills germs*
Instincts - *Natural intuitive power*
Sonorous - *Loud, deep*
Plausible - *Well-spoken*

Greatest Humour Stories

"It won't hurt us a bit," says Silver, "to get *acquainted* with a few finance kings. I kind of like the social way New York has with strangers."

The man Silver knew was named Klein. At three o'clock Klein brought his Wall Street friend to see us in Silver's room. "Mr. Morgan" looked some like his pictures, and he had a Turkish towel wrapped around his left foot, and he walked with a cane.

"Mr. Silver and Mr. Pescud," says Klein. "It sounds *superfluous*," says he, "to mention the name of the greatest financial -"

"Cut it out, Klein," says Mr. Morgan. "I'm glad to know you gents; I take great interest in the West. Klein tells me you're from Little Rock. I think I've a railroad or two out there somewhere. If either of you guys would like to deal a hand or two of stud poker I -"

"Now, Pierpont," cuts in Klein, "you forget!"

"Excuse me, gents!" says Morgan; "since I've had the gout so bad I sometimes play a social game of cards at my house. Neither of you never knew One-eyed Peters, did you, while you was around Little Rock? He lived in Seattle, New Mexico."

Before we could answer, Mr. Morgan hammers on the floor with his can and begins to walk up and down, swearing in a loud tone of voice.

"They have been *pounding* your stocks to-day on the Street, Pierpont?" asks Klein, smiling.

"Stocks! No!" roars Mr. Morgan. "It's that picture I sent an agent to Europe to buy. I just thought about it. He cabled me to-day that it ain't to be found in all Italy. I'd pay $50,000 to-morrow for that picture - yes, $75,000. I give the agent a la carte in purchasing it. I cannot understand why the art galleries will allow a De Vinchy to -"

"Why, Mr. Morgan," says klein; "I thought you owned all of the De Vinchy paintings."

"What is the picture like, Mr. Morgan?" asks Silver. "It must be as big as the side of the Flatiron Building."

"I'm afraid your art education is on the bum, Mr. Silver," says Morgan. "The picture is 27 inches by 42; and it is called 'Love's Idle Hour.' It represents a number of cloak models doing the two-step on the bank of a purple river. The *cablegram*

Acquainted
- *To make, more/less familiar*
Superfluous - *Being more than sufficient*
Pounding - *To strike repeatedly with great force*

said it might have been brought to this country. My collection will never be complete without that picture. Well, so long, gents; us financiers must keep early hours."

Mr. Morgan and Klein went away together in a cab. Me and Silver talked about how simple and unsuspecting great people was; and Silver said what a shame it would be to try to rob a man like Mr. Morgan; and I said I thought it would be rather imprudent, myself. Klein proposes a stroll after dinner; and me and him and Silver walks down toward Seventh Avenue to see the sights. Klein sees a pair of cuff links that instigate his admiration in a *pawnshop* window, and we all go in while he buys 'em.

After we got back to the hotel and Klein had gone, Silver jumps at me and waves his hands.

"Did you see it?" says he. "Did you see it, Billy?"

"What?" I asks.

"Why, that picture that Morgan wants. It's hanging in that pawnshop, behind the desk. I didn't say anything because Klein was there. It's the article sure as you live. The girls are as natural as paint can make them, all measuring 36 and 25 and 42 skirts, if they had any skirts, and they're doing a buck-and-wing on the bank of a river with the blues. What did Mr. Morgan say he'd give for it? Oh, don't make me tell you. They can't know what it is in that pawnshop."

When the pawnshop opened the next morning me and Silver was standing there as anxious as if we wanted to soak our Sunday suit to buy a drink. We sauntered inside, and began to look at watch-chains.

"That's a violent specimen of a chromo you've got up there," remarked Silver, casual, to the pawnbroker. "But I kind of *enthuse* over the girl with the shoulderblades and red bunting. Would an offer of $2.25 for it cause you to knock over any *fragile* articles of your stock in hurrying it off the nail?"

The pawnbroker smiles and goes on showing us plate watch-chains.

"That picture," says he, "was pledged a year ago by an Italian gentleman. I loaned him $500 on it. It is called 'Love's Idle Hour,' and it is by Leonardo de Vinchy. Two days ago the legal time expired, and it became an *unredeemed* pledge. Here is a style of chain that is worn a great deal now."

Pawnshop - *Premisens*
Enthuse - *To become enthusiastic*
Fragile - *Delicate*
Unredeemed - *To buy*

Greatest Humour Stories

At the end of half an hour, me and Silver paid the *pawn-broker* $2,000 and walked out with the picture. Silver got into a *cab* with it and started for Morgan's office. I goes to the hotel and waits for him. In two hours, Silver comes back.

"Did you see Mr. Morgan?" I asks. "How much did he pay you for it?"

Silver sits down and *fools* with a *tassel* on the table cover.

"I never exactly saw Mr. Morgan," he says, "because Mr. Morgan's been in Europe for a month. But what's worrying me, Billy, is this: The *department stores* have all got that same picture on sale, framed, for $3.48. And they charge $3.50 for the frame alone - that's what I can't understand."

Cab - *Taxi*
Tassel - *A pendant ornament tied to a piece*
Department stores - *Big retail shops, grocery of thread*

Food For Thought

Mr. Morgan was one of the few finance kings of New York according to Silver. What did Morgan want to buy and how did he fool Billy and Silver (both) at the end of the story? Can you suggest a moral for the story? Also give appropriate reasons for your suggestion.

An Understanding

Q. 1. Who was Montague Silver and where did he meet Billy? What did he say about New York during their conversation in Little Rock?
Ans. _____
_____
_____
_____
_____

Q. 2. Why did Billy leave for New York? How did he meet Silver there and where was Silver staying in New York?
Ans. _____
_____
_____
_____
_____

Q. 3. "There's more ways of getting money from these metropolitan hayseeds," says Silver " than there is of cooking rice in Charleston S.C. They'll bite at anything." What do you think Silver meant by saying the above words?
Ans. _____
_____
_____
_____
_____

Q. 4. How much capital did Billy have at the end and how much did Silver have? What did Silver suggest Billy with their joint capital?
Ans. _____
_____
_____
_____
_____

Adrian

~ Saki

A Chapter in Acclimatization

HIs *baptismal* register spoke of him pessimistically as John Henry, but he had left that behind with the other maladies of infancy, and his friends knew him under the front-name of Adrian. His mother lived in Bethnal Green, which was not altogether his fault; one can discourage too much history in one's family, but one cannot always prevent geography. And, after all, the Bethnal Green habit has this virtue - that it is ***seldom transmitted*** to the next generation. Adrian lived in a roomlet which came under the auspicious constellation of W.

How he lived was to a great extent a mystery even to himself; his struggle for existence probably coincided in many material details with the rather dramatic accounts he gave of it to sympathetic acquaintances. All that is definitely known is that he now and then emerged from the struggle to dine at the Ritz or Carlton, correctly garbed and with a correctly critical appetite. On these occasions he was usually the guest of Lucas Croyden, an amiable worldling, who had three thousand a year and a taste for introducing impossible people to *irreproachable* cookery. Like most men who combine three thousand a year with an uncertain digestion, Lucas was a Socialist, and he argued that you cannot hope to elevate the masses until you have brought plovers' eggs into their lives and taught them to appreciate the difference between coupe Jacques and MacEdoine de fruits. His friends pointed out that it was a doubtful kindness to initiate a boy from behind a *drapery* counter into the *blessedness* of the higher catering, to which Lucas invariably replied that all kindnesses were doubtful. Which was perhaps true.

It was after one of his Adrian evenings that Lucas met his aunt, Mrs. Mebberley, at a fashionable teashop, where the lamp of family life is still kept burning and you meet relatives who might otherwise have slipped your memory.

"Who was that good-looking boy who was dining with you last night?" she asked. "He looked much too nice to be thrown away upon you."

Baptismal - *A trying*
Seldom - *Rauely*
Transmitted - *To spread*
Drapery - *Coverings*

Susan Mebberley was a charming woman, but she was also an aunt.

"Who are his people?" she continued, when the *protege's* name (revised version) had been given her.

"His mother lives at Beth--"

Lucas checked himself on the threshold of what was perhaps a social ***indiscretion***.

"Beth? Where is it? It sounds like Asia Minor. Is she mixed up with Consular people?"

"Oh, no. Her work lies among the poor."

This was a side-slip into truth. The mother of Adrian was employed in a laundry.

"I see," said Mrs. Mebberley, "mission work of some sort. And meanwhile the boy has no one to look after him. It's obviously my duty to see that he doesn't come to harm. Bring him to call on me."

"My dear Aunt Susan," ***expostulated*** Lucas, "I really know very little about him. He may not be at all nice, you know, on further acquaintance."

"He has delightful hair and a weak mouth. I shall take him with me to Homburg or Cairo."

"It's the maddest thing I ever heard of," said Lucas angrily.

"Well, there is a strong strain of madness in our family. If you haven't noticed it yourself all your friends must have."

"One is so dreadfully under everybody's eyes at Homburg. At least you might give him a preliminary trial at Etretat."

"And be surrounded by Americans trying to talk French? No, thank you. I love Americans, but not when they try to talk French. What a blessing it is that they never try to talk English. Tomorrow at five you can bring your young friend to call on me."

And Lucas, realizing that Susan Mebberley was a woman as well as an aunt, saw that she would have to be allowed to have her own way.

Adrian was duly carried abroad under the Mebberley wing; but as a ***reluctant concession*** to sanity Homburg and other inconveniently fashionable resorts were given a wide berth, and the Mebberley establishment planted itself down in the best hotel at Dohledorf, an Alpine ***townlet*** somewhere at the back of the Engadine. It was the usual kind of resort, with the usual type of visitors, that one finds over the greater part

Protege - *A person under the patronage, protection*
Indiscretion - *Imprudence*
Expostulated - *A argue*
Reluctant - *Unwilling*
Townlet - *A small town*

of Switzerland during the summer season, but to Adrian it was all unusual. The mountain air, the certainty of regular and abundant meals, and in particular the social atmosphere, affected him much as the *indiscriminating fervour* of a forcing-house might affect a weed that had strayed within its limits. He had been brought up in a world where *breakages* were regarded as crimes and expiated as such; it was something new and altogether *exhilarating* to find that you were considered rather amusing if you smashed things in the right manner and at the recognised hours. Susan Mebberley had expressed the intention of showing Adrian a bit of the world; the particular bit of the world represented by Dohledorf began to be shown a good deal of Adrian.

Lucas got occasional glimpses of the Alpine sojourn, not from his aunt or Adrian, but from the industrious pen of Clovis, who was also moving as a satellite in the Mebberley constellation.

"The entertainment which Susan got up last night ended in disaster. I thought it would. The Grobmayer child, a particularly *loathsome* five-year-old, had appeared as 'Bubbles' during the early part of the evening, and been put to bed during the interval. Adrian watched his opportunity and kidnapped it when the nurse was downstairs, and introduced it during the second half of the entertainment, thinly disguised as a performing pig. It certainly looked very like a pig, and grunted and *slobbered* just like the real article; no one knew exactly what it was, but every one said it was awfully clever, especially the Grobmayers. At the third curtain Adrian pinched it too hard, and it yelled 'Marmar'! I am supposed to be good at descriptions, but don't ask me to describe the sayings and doings of the Grobmayers at that moment; it was like one of the angrier Psalms set to Strauss's music. We have moved to an hotel higher up the valley."

Clovis's next letter arrived five days later, and was written from the Hotel Steinbock.

"We left the Hotel Victoria this morning. It was fairly comfortable and quiet - at least there was an air of repose about it when we arrived. Before we had been in residence twenty-four hours most of the repose had vanished 'like a dutiful bream,' as Adrian expressed it. However, nothing *unduly outrageous* happened till last night, when Adrian had a fit of *insomnia* and amused himself by *unscrewing* and transposing all the bedroom numbers on his floor. He transferred the bathroom label to the adjoining bedroom door, which happened to be that of Frau

Indiscriminating - *Differentiating*
Fervour - *Zest zeal*
Breakages - *To enliven*
Exhilarating - *Disguesting*
Loathsome - *To let saliva run from the mouth*
Slobbered -

Hofrath Schilling, and this morning from seven o'clock onwards the old lady had a stream of involuntary visitors; she was too horrified and scandalised it seems to get up and lock her door. The would-be bathers flew back in confusion to their rooms, and, of course, the change of numbers led them astray again, and the corridor gradually filled with panic-stricken, scantily robed humans, dashing wildly about like rabbits in a ***ferret-infested warren.*** It took nearly an hour before the guests were all sorted into their respective rooms, and the Frau Hofrath's condition was still causing some anxiety when we left. Susan is beginning to look a little worried. She can't very well turn the boy adrift, as he hasn't got any money, and she can't send him to his people as she doesn't know where they are. Adrian says his mother moves about a good deal and he's lost her address. Probably, if the truth were known, he's had a row at home. So many boys nowadays seem to think that quarrelling with one's family is a recognised occupation."

Lucas's next communication from the travellers took the form of a telegram from Mrs. Mebberley herself. It was sent "reply prepaid," and consisted of a single sentence: "In Heaven's name, where is Beth?"

Insomnia - *Sleeplessness*
unscrewing - *To unfasten*
Warren - *A place where rabbits breed*

Food For Thought

Adrian said to Mrs. Mebberley that he had lost his mother's address as she moved about a great deal. Adrian had no money and nowhere to go. Why do you think Lucas's aunt, Mrs. Mebberley didn't want to keep Adrian with her any longer? Also, why do you think Adrian had fits of insomnia and was very mischievous and troublesome?

An Understanding

Q. 1. Who was Adrian? What was his actual name? Where did he live presently and where was his mother?
Ans. _____
_____
_____
_____
_____

Q. 2. Who was Lucas and what was his belief?
Ans. _____
_____
_____
_____

Q. 3. Where did Lucas meet Mrs. Mebberley? What relationship did Lucas share with Mrs. Mebberley? Give a brief character sketch of Mrs. Mebberley.
Ans. _____
_____
_____
_____
_____

Q. 4. Why did Mrs. Mebberley want to meet Adrian? Why was Lucas reluctant on introducing Adrian to his aunt, Mrs. Mebberley? What did Mrs. Mebberley propose to do with Adrian?
Ans. _____
_____
_____
_____
_____

One Summer Night
– Ambrose Bierce

The fact that Henry Armstrong was buried did not seem to him to prove that he was dead: he had always been a hard man to convince. That he really was buried, the testimony of his senses **compelled** him to admit. His posture -- flat upon his back, with his hands crossed upon his stomach and tied with something that he easily broke without profitably altering the situation -- the strict confinement of his entire person, the black darkness and **profound** silence, made a body of evidence impossible to **controvert** and he accepted it without **cavil**.

But dead -- no; he was only very, very ill. He had, **withal**, the invalid's apathy and did not greatly concern himself about the uncommon fate that had been allotted to him. No philosopher was he -- just a plain, commonplace person gifted, for the time being, with a pathological **indifference**: the organ that he feared consequences with was torpid. So, with no particular **apprehension** for his immediate future, he fell asleep and all was peace with Henry Armstrong.

But something was going on overhead. It was a dark summer night, shot through with infrequent shimmers of lightning silently firing a cloud lying low in the west and **portending** a storm. These brief, **stammering** illuminations brought out with ghastly distinctness the monuments and headstones of the cemetery and seemed to set them dancing. It was not a night in which any credible witness was likely to be straying about a cemetery, so the three men who were there, digging into the grave of Henry Armstrong, felt reasonably secure.

Two of them were young students from a medical college a few miles away; the third was a gigantic negro known as Jess. For many years, Jess had been employed about the cemetery as a man-of-all-work and it was his favourite pleasantry that he knew 'every soul in the place.' From the nature of what he was now doing it was **inferable** that the place was not so populous as its register may have shown it to be.

Outside the wall, at the part of the grounds farthest from the public road, were a horse and a light wagon, waiting.

The work of **excavation** was not difficult: the earth with which the grave had been loosely filled a few hours before offered little resistance and was soon thrown out. Removal of the

Torpid - *Inactive*
Withal - *Inspited of all*
Cavil - *A trivila objection*
Controvert - *To aruge*
Inferable - *To guess*

casket from its box was less easy, but it was taken out, for it was a perquisite of Jess, who carefully unscrewed the cover and laid it aside, exposing the body in black trousers and white shirt. At that instant, the air sprang to flame, a cracking shock of thunder shook the stunned world and Henry Armstrong *tranquilly* sat up. With *inarticulate* cries, the men fled in terror, each in a different direction. For nothing on earth could two of them have been persuaded to return. But Jess was of another breed.

In the grey of the morning, the two students, *pallid* and *haggard* from anxiety and with the terror of their adventure still beating *tumultuously* in their blood, met at the medical college.

'You saw it?' cried one.

'God! yes -- what are we to do?'

They went around to the rear of the building, where they saw a horse, attached to a light wagon, *hitched* to a *gatepost* near the door of the dissecting-room. Mechanically they entered the room. On a bench in the *obscurity* sat the negro Jess. He rose, grinning, all eyes and teeth.

'I'm waiting for my pay,' he said.

Stretched naked on a long table lay the body of Henry Armstrong, the head *defiled* with blood and clay from a blow with a spade.

Inarticulate - *Lacking the ability to express oneself*
Casket - *A coffin*
Haggard - *Wild*
Tumultuously - *Highly agrtated*
Obscurity - *Uncertainty*

Food For Thought

" I'm waiting for my pay." Who said this and why? What kind of pay was the speaker expecting from the two young students from a medical college?

An Understanding

Q. 1. Was Henry Armstrong dead or alive? Why was he buried if he was not dead?
Ans. _____

Q. 2. Who were the three men digging a grave for Henry Armstrong on that cloudy summer night? Also describe the weather at that time.
Ans. _____

Q. 3. The work of excavation was not difficult and Armstrong lay very peacefully in black trouser's ad white shirt inside the coffin. What suddenly happened early in the morning? Why did the two medical students digging his grave run away?
Ans. _____

Q. 4. Why didn't the third person, who was a Negro, called Jess flee? What happened next?
Ans. _____

The Ransom Of Red Chief
~ O. Henry

IT looked like a good thing: but wait till I tell you. We were down South, in Alabama - Bill Driscoll and myself- when this kidnapping idea struck us. It was, as Bill afterward expressed it, "during a moment of temporary mental aparition"; but we didn't find that out till later.

There was a town down there, as flat as a flannel-cake, and called Summit, of course. It contained inhabitants of as undeleterious and self-satisfied a class of peasantry as ever clustered around a Maypole.

Bill and me had a joint capital of about six hundred dollars, and we needed just two thousand dollars more to pull off a *fraudulent* town-lot scheme in Western Illinois with. We talked it over on the front steps of the hotel. **Philoprogenitiveness**, says we, is strong in semi-rural communities therefore, and for other reasons, a kidnapping project ought to do better there than in the radius of newspapers that send reporters out in plain clothes to stir up talk about such things. We knew that Summit couldn't get after us with anything stronger than constables and, maybe, some ***lackadaisical bloodhounds*** and a ***diatribe*** or two in the Weekly Farmers' Budget. So, it looked good.

We selected for our victim the only child of a prominent citizen named Ebenezer Dorset. The father was respectable and tight, a **mortgage** fancier and a stern, upright collection-plate passer and foreclose. The kid was a boy of ten, with bas-relief *freckles*, and hair the colour of the cover of the magazine you buy at the news-stand when you want to catch a train. Bill and me figured that Ebenezer would melt down for a ransom of two thousand dollars to a cent. But wait till I tell you.

About two miles from Summit was a little mountain, covered with a dense cedar brake. On the rear elevation of this mountain was a cave. There we stored provisions.

One evening after sundown, we drove in a ***buggy*** past old Dorset's house. The kid was in the street, throwing rocks at a kitten on the opposite fence.

"Hey, little boy!" says Bill, "would you like to have a bag of candy and a nice ride?"

Clustered - *Crowded*
Fraudulnt - *Put together*
Lackadaisical - *Without interest*
Diatribe - *A bitter, sharp attacj*
Mortgage - *To pledge as security*
Trickles - *To flow*
Buggy - *A light*

Greatest   Humour   Stories

The boy catches Bill neatly in the eye with a piece of brick.

"That will cost the old man an extra five hundred dollars," says Bill, climbing over the wheel.

That boy put up a fight like a welter-weight cinnamon bear; but, at last, we got him down in the bottom of the buggy and drove away. We took him up to the cave, and I hitched the horse in the cedar brake. After dark I drove the buggy to the little village, three miles away, where we had hired it, and walked back to the mountain.

Bill was pasting *court-plaster* over the scratches and bruises on his features. There was a fire burning behind the big rock at the entrance of the cave, and the boy was watching a pot of boiling coffee, with two *buzzard* tailfeathers stuck in his red hair. He points a stick at me when I come up, and says:

"Ha! cursed paleface, do you dare to enter the camp of Red Chief, the terror of the plains?"

"He's all right now," says Bill, rolling up his trousers and examining some bruises on his *shins*. "We're playing Indian. We're making Buffalo Bill's show look like magic-lantern views of Palestine in the town hall. I'm Old Hank, the Trapper, Red Chief's captive, and I'm to be scalped at daybreak. By Geronimo! that kid can kick hard."

Yes, sir, that boy seemed to be having the time of his life. The fun of camping out in a cave had made him forget that he was a captive himself. He immediately christened me Snake-eye, the Spy, and announced that, when his braves returned from the warpath, I was to be *broiled* at the stake at the rising of the sun.

Then we had supper; and he filled his mouth full of *bacon* and bread and gravy, and began to talk. He made a during-dinner speech something like this:

"I like this fine. I never camped out before; but I had a pet 'possum once, and I was nine last birthday. I hate to go to school. Rats ate up sixteen of Jimmy Talbot's aunt's *speckled* hen's eggs. Are there any real Indians in these woods? I want some more gravy. Does the trees moving make the wind blow? We had five puppies. What makes your nose so red, Hank? My father has lots of money. Are the stars hot? I whipped Ed Walker twice, Saturday. I don't like girls. You dassent catch toads unless with a string. Do oxen make any noise? Why are oranges round? Have you got beds to sleep on in this cave?

Buzzard - *Senseless*
Shins - *The front part of the leg from the knee to the ankle*
Broiled - *To cook by direct heat*
Bacon - *Meat of a pig*
Speckled - *Spots/marks on the skin*

Amos Murray has got six toes. A parrot can talk, but a monkey or a fish can't. How many does it take to make twelve?"

Every few minutes he would remember that he was a pesky redskin, and pick up his stick rifle and *tiptoe* to the mouth of the cave to rubber for the scouts of the hated paleface. Now and then he would let out a warwhoop that made Old Hank the Trapper, shiver. That boy had Bill terrorised from the start.

"Red Chief," says I to the kid, "would you like to go home?"

"Aw, what for?" says he. "I don't have any fun at home. I hate to go to school. I like to camp out. You won't take me back home again, Snake-eye, will you?"

"Not right away," says I. "We'll stay here in the cave a while."

"All right!" says he. "That'll be fine. I never had such fun in all my life."

We went to bed about eleven o'clock. We spread down some wide blankets and quilts and put Red Chief between us. We weren't afraid he'd run away. He kept us awake for three hours, jumping up and reaching for his rifle and screeching: "Hist! pard," in mine and Bill's ears, as the fancied *crackle* of a twig or the rustle of a leaf revealed to his young imagination the stealthy approach of the *outlaw* band. At last, I fell into a troubled sleep, and dreamed that I had been kidnapped and chained to a tree by a *ferocious* pirate with red hair.

Just at daybreak, I was awakened by a series of awful screams from Bill. They weren't yells, or howls, or shouts, or whoops, or yawps, such as you'd expect from a manly set of vocal organs - they were simply indecent, terrifying, humiliating screams, such as women emit when they see ghosts or caterpillars. It's an awful thing to hear a strong, *desperate*, fat man scream *incontinently* in a cave at daybreak.

I jumped up to see what the matter was. Red Chief was sitting on Bill's chest, with one hand *twined* in Bill's hair. In the other he had the sharp case-knife we used for slicing bacon; and he was industriously and realistically trying to take Bill's scalp, according to the sentence that had been pronounced upon him the evening before.

I got the knife away from the kid and made him lie down again. But, from that moment, Bill's spirit was broken. He laid

Tiptoe - *To move slowly*
Ferocious - *Fierce, very cruel*
Incontinently - *Immediately*
Twined - *Coiled/twisted*

Greatest Humour Stories

down on his side of the bed, but he never closed an eye again in sleep as long as that boy was with us. I dozed off for a while, but along toward sun-up I remembered that Red Chief had said I was to be burned at the stake at the rising of the sun. I wasn't nervous or afraid; but I sat up and lit my pipe and leaned against a rock.

"What you getting up so soon for, Sam?" asked Bill.

"Me?" says I. "Oh, I got a kind of a pain in my shoulder. I thought sitting up would rest it."

"You're a liar!" says Bill. "You're afraid. You was to be burned at sunrise, and you was afraid he'd do it. And he would, too, if he could find a match. Ain't it awful, Sam? Do you think anybody will pay out money to get a little imp like that back home?"

"Sure," said I. "A rowdy kid like that is just the kind that parents dote on. Now, you and the Chief get up and cook breakfast, while I go up on the top of this mountain and **reconnoitre**."

I went up on the peak of the little mountain and ran my eye over the **contiguous vicinity.** Over toward Summit I expected to see the sturdy **yeomanry** of the village armed with scythes and **pitchforks** beating the countryside for the dastardly kidnappers. But what I saw was a peaceful landscape dotted with one man ploughing with a dun mule. Nobody was dragging the creek; no couriers dashed hither and yon, bringing tidings of no news to the **distracted** parents. There was a **sylvan** attitude of somnolent sleepiness pervading that section of the external outward surface of Alabama that lay exposed to my view. "Perhaps," says I to myself, "it has not yet been discovered that the wolves have borne away the tender lambkin from the fold. Heaven help the wolves!" says I, and I went down the mountain to breakfast.

When I got to the cave I found Bill backed up against the side of it, breathing hard, and the boy threatening to smash him with a rock half as big as a coconut.

"He put a red-hot boiled potato down my back," explained Bill, "and then mashed it with his foot; and I boxed his ears. Have you got a gun about you, Sam?"

I took the rock away from the boy and kind of patched up the argument. "I'll fix you," says the kid to Bill. "No man ever yet struck the Red Chief but what he got paid for it. You better beware!"

Reconnoitre - *To survey/inspect*
Contiguous - *In close proximity*
Vicinity - *Surrounding area*
Distracted - *Attention diverted*

After breakfast the kid takes a piece of leather with strings wrapped around it out of his pocket and goes outside the cave *unwinding* it.

"What's he up to now?" says Bill, anxiously. "You don't think he'll run away, do you, Sam?"

"No fear of it," says I. "He don't seem to be much of a home body. But we've got to fix up some plan about the ransom. There don't seem to be much excitement around Summit on account of his disappearance; but maybe they haven't realised yet that he's gone. His folks may think he's spending the night with Aunt Jane or one of the neighbours. Anyhow, he'll be missed to-day. To-night we must get a message to his father demanding the two thousand dollars for his return."

Just then we heard a kind of *war-whoop,* such as David might have emitted when he knocked out the champion Goliath. It was a sling that Red Chief had pulled out of his pocket, and he was whirling it around his head.

I dodged, and heard a heavy thud and a kind of a sigh from Bill, like a horse gives out when you take his saddle off. A *niggerhead* rock the size of an egg had caught Bill just behind his left ear. He loosened himself all over and fell in the fire across the frying pan of hot water for washing the dishes. I dragged him out and poured cold water on his head for half an hour.

By and by, Bill sits up and feels behind his ear and says: "Sam, do you know who my favourite Biblical character is?"

"Take it easy," says I. "You'll come to your senses presently."

"King Herod," says he. "You won't go away and leave me here alone, will you, Sam?"

I went out and caught that boy and shook him until his *freckles rattled.*

"If you don't behave," says I, "I'll take you straight home. Now, are you going to be good, or not?"

"I was only funning," says he *sullenly*. "I didn't mean to hurt Old Hank. But what did he hit me for? I'll behave, Snake-eye, if you won't send me home, and if you'll let me play the Black Scout to-day."

"I don't know the game," says I. "That's for you and Mr. Bill to decide. He's your playmate for the day. I'm going

War-whoop - *A yell uttered while attacking during war*
Niggerhead - *A strong, black chewing*
Freckles - *Small brownish spots on skin*
Rattled - *To talk rapidly*
Sullenly - *Gloomily, morose*

away for a while, on business. Now, you come in and make friends with him and say you are sorry for hurting him, or home you go, at once."

I made him and Bill shake hands, and then I took Bill aside and told him I was going to Poplar Cove, a little village three miles from the cave, and find out what I could about how the kidnapping had been regarded in Summit. Also, I thought it best to send a *peremptory* letter to old man Dorset that day, demanding the ransom and dictating how it should be paid.

"You know, Sam," says Bill, "I've stood by you without batting an eye in earthquakes, fire and flood - in poker games, dynamite *outrages*, police raids, train robberies and cyclones. I never lost my nerve yet till we kidnapped that two-legged skyrocket of a kid. He's got me going. You won't leave me long with him, will you, Sam?"

"I'll be back some time this afternoon," says I. "You must keep the boy amused and quiet till I return. And now we'll write the letter to old Dorset."

Bill and I got paper and pencil and worked on the letter while Red Chief, with a blanket wrapped around him, *strutted* up and down, guarding the mouth of the cave. Bill begged me tearfully to make the ransom fifteen hundred dollars instead of two thousand. "I ain't attempting," says he, "to decry the celebrated moral aspect of parental affection, but we're dealing with humans, and it ain't human for anybody to give up two thousand dollars for that forty-pound chunk of freckled wildcat. I'm willing to take a chance at fifteen hundred dollars. You can charge the difference up to me."

So, to relieve Bill, I acceded, and we *collaborated* a letter that ran this way:

Ebenezer Dorset, Esq.:

We have your boy concealed in a place far from Summit. It is useless for you or the most skilful detectives to attempt to find him. Absolutely, the only terms on which you can have him restored to you are these: We demand fifteen hundred dollars in large bills for his return; the money to be left at midnight to-night at the same spot and in the same box as your reply - as hereinafter described. If you agree to these terms, send your answer in writing by a solitary messenger to-night at half-past eight o'clock. After crossing Owl Creek, on the road to Poplar

Peremptory
- Leaving no opportunity for refusal
Outrages *- Insutts*
Strutted *- To walk with vain/pride*
Collaborated *- To work with one another*

Cove, there are three large trees about a hundred yards apart, close to the fence of the wheat field on the right-hand side. At the bottom of the fence-post, opposite the third tree, will be found a small **pasteboard box.**

The messenger will place the answer in this box and return immediately to Summit.

If you attempt any **treachery** or fail to comply with our demand as stated, you will never see your boy again.

If you pay the money as demanded, he will be returned to you safe and well within three hours. These terms are final, and if you do not accede to them no further communication will be attempted.

TWO DESPERATE MEN.

I addressed this letter to Dorset, and put it in my pocket. As I was about to start, the kid comes up to me and says:

"Aw, Snake-eye, you said I could play the Black Scout while you was gone."

"Play it, of course," says I. "Mr. Bill will play with you. What kind of a game is it?"

"I'm the Black Scout," says Red Chief, "and I have to ride to the **stockade** to warn the settlers that the Indians are coming. I'm tired of playing Indian myself. I want to be the Black Scout."

"All right," says I. "It sounds harmless to me. I guess Mr. Bill will help you foil the pesky savages."

"What am I to do?" asks Bill, looking at the kid suspiciously.

"You are the hoss," says Black Scout. "Get down on your hands and knees. How can I ride to the stockade without a hoss?"

"You'd better keep him interested," said I, "till we get the scheme going. Loosen up."

Bill gets down on his all fours, and a look comes in his eye like a rabbit's when you catch it in a trap.

"How far is it to the stockade, kid?" he asks, in a husky manner of voice.

"Ninety miles," says the Black Scout. "And you have to hump yourself to get there on time. Whoa, now!"

The Black Scout jumps on Bill's back and digs his heels in his side.

Stockage - *An enclosure/barrier*
Hump - *A rounded protuberance*
Suspiciously - *Doubtful dubious*

"For Heaven's sake," says Bill, "hurry back, Sam, as soon as you can. I wish we hadn't made the ransom more than a thousand. Say, you quit kicking me or I 'll get up and warm you good."

I walked over to Poplar Cove and sat around the post office and store, talking with the chawbacons that came in to trade. One *whiskerand* says that he hears Summit is all upset on account of Elder Ebenezer Dorset's boy having been lost or stolen. That was all I wanted to know. I bought some smoking tobacco, referred casually to the price of black-eyed peas, posted my letter *surreptitiously* and came away. The postmaster said the mail-carrier would come by in an hour to take the mail on to Summit.

When I got back to the cave Bill and the boy were not to be found. I explored the *vicinity* of the cave, and risked a yodel or two, but there was no response.

So I lighted my pipe and sat down on a mossy bank to await developments.

In about half an hour I heard the bushes rustle, and Bill wabbled out into the little glade in front of the cave. Behind him was the kid, stepping softly like a scout, with a broad grin on his face. Bill stopped, took off his hat and wiped his face with a red handkerchief. The kid stopped about eight feet behind him.

"Sam," says Bill, "I suppose you'll think I'm a renegade, but I couldn't help it. I'm a grown person with masculine proclivities and habits of self-defence, but there is a time when all systems of *egotism* and *predominance* fail. The boy is gone. I have sent him home. All is off. There was martyrs in old times," goes on Bill, "that suffered death rather than give up the particular graft they enjoyed. None of 'em ever was subjugated to such supernatural tortures as I have been. I tried to be faithful to our articles of depredation; but there came a limit."

"What's the trouble, Bill?" I asks him.

"I was rode," says Bill, "the ninety miles to the stockade, not barring an inch. Then, when the settlers was rescued, I was given oats. Sand ain't a *palatable* substitute. And then, for an hour I had to try to explain to him why there was nothin' in holes, how a road can run both ways and what makes the grass green. I tell you, Sam, a human can only stand so much. I takes him by the neck of his clothes and drags him down the

Whisked - *Having whiskers/hair on the face*
Surreptitiously - *Secretly*
Egotism - *Boastfullness*
Palatable - *Tasty, acceptable*

mountain. On the way he kicks my legs black-and-blue from the knees down; and I've got two or three bites on my thumb and hand *cauterised*.

"But he's gone" - continues Bill - "gone home. I showed him the road to Summit and kicked him about eight feet nearer there at one kick. I'm sorry we lose the ransom; but it was either that or Bill Driscoll to the madhouse."

Bill is *puffing* and blowing, but there is a look of *ineffable* peace and growing content on his rose-pink features.

"Bill," says I, "there isn't any heart disease in your family, is there?"

"No," says Bill, "nothing chronic except malaria and accidents. Why?"

"Then you might turn around," says I, "and have a look behind you."

Bill turns and sees the boy, and loses his complexion and sits down plump on the ground and begins to pluck aimlessly at grass and little sticks. For an hour I was afraid for his mind. And then I told him that my scheme was to put the whole job through immediately and that we would get the ransom and be off with it by midnight if old Dorset fell in with our proposition. So Bill braced up enough to give the kid a weak sort of a smile and a promise to play the Russian in a Japanese war with him as soon as he felt a little better.

I had a scheme for collecting that ransom without danger of being caught by *counterplots* that ought to commend itself to professional kidnappers. The tree under which the answer was to be left - and the money later on - was close to the road fence with big, bare fields on all sides. If a gang of constables should be watching for any one to come for the note they could see him a long way off crossing the fields or in the road. But no, sirree! At half-past eight, I was up in that tree as well hidden as a tree toad, waiting for the messenger to arrive.

Exactly on time, a half-grown boy rides up the road on a bicycle, locates the pasteboard box at the foot of the fencepost, slips a folded piece of paper into it and pedals away again back toward Summit.

I waited an hour and then concluded the thing was square. I slid down the tree, got the note, slipped along the fence till I struck the woods, and was back at the cave in another half an hour. I opened the note, got near the lantern and read it to

Cauterised - *To burn with a hot iron*
Puffing - *Inhaling/exhaling*
Ineffable *-Inexpressible*
Counterplots - *To oppose*

Bill. It was written with a pen in a crabbed hand, and the sum and substance of it was this:

Two Desperate Men.

Gentlemen: I received your letter to-day by post, in regard to the ransom you ask for the return of my son. I think you are a little high in your demands, and I hereby make you a counter-proposition, which I am inclined to believe you will accept. You bring Johnny home and pay me two hundred and fifty dollars in cash, and I agree to take him off your hands. You had better come at night, for the neighbours believe he is lost, and I couldn't be responsible for what they would do to anybody they saw bringing him back.

Very respectfully,
Ebenezer Dorset.

"Great pirates of Penzance!" says I; "of all the **impudent** - "

But I glanced at Bill, and hesitated. He had the most appealing look in his eyes I ever saw on the face of a dumb or a talking brute.

"Sam," says he, "what's two hundred and fifty dollars, after all? We've got the money. One more night of this kid will send me to a bed in Bedlam. Besides being a thorough gentleman, I think Mr. Dorset is a **spendthrift** for making us such a liberal offer. You ain't going to let the chance go, are you?"

"Tell you the truth, Bill," says I, "this little he ewe lamb has somewhat got on my nerves too. We'll take him home, pay the ransom and make our get-away."

We took him home that night. We got him to go by telling him that his father had bought a silver-mounted rifle and a pair of **moccasins** for him, and we were going to hunt bears the next day.

It was just twelve o'clock when we knocked at Ebenezer's front door. Just at the moment when I should have been abstracting the fifteen hundred dollars from the box under the tree, according to the original proposition, Bill was counting out two hundred and fifty dollars into Dorset's hand.

When the kid found out we were going to leave him at home he started up a howl like a **calliope** and fastened himself as tight as a leech to Bill's leg. His father peeled him away gradually, like a porous plaster.

Impudent - *Shameless, immodest*
Spendthrift - *Extravagant*
Moccasins - *Hard-soled shoes*
Calliope - *A steam-whistle organ in music with a loud sound*

"How long can you hold him?" asks Bill.

"I'm not as strong as I used to be," says old Dorset, "but I think I can promise you ten minutes."

"Enough," says Bill. "In ten minutes I shall cross the Central, Southern and Middle Western States, and be legging it *trippingly* for the Canadian border."

And, as dark as it was, and as fat as Bill was, and as good a runner as I am, he was a good mile and a half out of Summit before I could catch up with him.

Trippingly -

Food For Thought

Do you think that this story, 'The Ransom of the Red Chief' written by O.Henry in 1910 is one of his best works and one of the most humourous stories of the world? Give reasons for your answer.

An Understanding

Q. 1. Who were Sam and Bill? How did a kidnapping idea struck them? Why did they select the child of Ebenezer Dorest?
Ans. _____
_____
_____
_____
_____

Q. 2. Who was the 'Red Chief' in the story? What was his real name and how did he behave with his kidnappers, Same and Bill? Describe briefly.
Ans. _____
_____
_____
_____
_____

Q. 3. Bill and Sam had decided and wrote a letter secretly to Ebenezer Dorset, the father of the so called 'Red Chief'. What was the amount of the ransom demanded by them? Did they get the money? What happened actually?
Ans. _____
_____
_____
_____
_____

Q. 4. "I'm not as strong as I used to be, but I think I can promise you ten minutes". Who said these words to whom? What would happen in ten minutes? Narrate the events that follow briefly.
Ans. _____
_____
_____
_____
_____

The Legend Of Sleepy Hollow
~ Washington Irving

IN the bosom of one of those spacious coves which indent the eastern shore of the Hudson, at that broad expansion of the river **denominated** by the ancient Dutch navigators the Tappan Zee, and where they always prudently shortened sail and implored the protection of Saint Nicholas, there lies a small market town which is generally known by the name of Tarry Town. This name was given by the good housewives of the adjacent country from the inveterate propensity of their husbands to linger about the village tavern on market days. Not far from this village, perhaps about two miles, there is a little valley among high hills which is one of the quietest places in the whole world. A small brook **murmurs** through it and, with the occasional whistle of a quail or tapping of a woodpecker, is almost the only sound that ever breaks the uniform **tranquillity**.

From the listless repose of the place, this sequestered glen has long been known by the name of Sleepy Hollow. Some say that the place was **bewitched** during the early days of the Dutch settlement; others, that an old Indian chief, the wizard of his tribe, held his powwows there before the country was discovered by Master Hendrick Hudson.

Certain it is, the place still continues under the sway of some witching power that holds a spell over the minds of the **descendants** of the original settlers. They are given to all kinds of marvelous beliefs, are subject to **trances** and visions, and frequently hear music and voices in the air. The whole neighborhood abounds with local tales, haunted spots, and twilight **superstitions**.

The dominant spirit that haunts this enchanted region is the apparition of a figure on horseback without a head. It is said to be the ghost of a Hessian trooper, whose head had been carried away by a cannonball in some nameless battle during the Revolutionary War, and who is ever seen by the countryfolk, hurrying along in the gloom of the night as if on the wings of the wind. Historians of those parts allege that the body of the **trooper** having been buried in the yard of a church

Denominated - *Designated*
Bewitched - *To fascinate*
Descendants - *Offsprings*
Trances - *Half unconscious state*
Trooper - *A horse-cavalry soldier*

at no great distance, the ghost rides forth to the scene of battle in nightly quest of his head; and that the rushing speed with which he sometimes passes along the Hollow is owing to his being in a hurry to get back to the churchyard before daybreak. The specter is known, at all the country firesides, by the name of the Headless Horseman of Sleepy Hollow.

It is remarkable that this visionary *propensity* is not confined to native *inhabitants* of this little retired Dutch valley, but is unconsciously *imbibed* by everyone who resides there for a time. However wide-awake they may have been before they entered that sleepy region, they are sure, in a little time, to inhale the witching influence of the air and begin to grow imaginative, to dream dreams, and see apparitions.

In this by-place of nature there abode, some thirty years since, a worthy *wight* of the name of Ichabod Crane, a native of Connecticut, who "*tarried*" in Sleepy Hollow for the purpose of instructing the children of the vicinity. He was tall and exceedingly *lank*, with narrow shoulders, long arms and legs, hands that dangled a mile out of his sleeves, and feet that might have served for *shovels*. His head was small, and flat at top, with huge ears, large green glassy eyes, and a long *snipe* nose, so that it looked like a weathercock perched upon his spindle neck, to tell which way the wind blew. To see him striding along on a windy day, with his clothes bagging and fluttering about him, one might have mistaken him for some scarecrow *eloped* from a cornfield.

His schoolhouse was a low building of one large room, rudely constructed of logs. It stood in a rather lonely but pleasant situation, just at the foot of a woody hill, with a brook running close by, and a formidable birch tree growing at one end of it. From hence the low murmur of his pupils' voices, conning over their lessons, might be heard on a drowsy summer's day, interrupted now and then by the voice of the master in a tone of menace or command; or by the *appalling* sound of the birch as he urged some wrongheaded Dutch urchin along the flowery path of knowledge. All this he called "doing his duty," and he never inflicted a *chastisement* without following it by the assurance, so consolatory to the smarting urchin, that "he would remember it, and thank him for it the longest day he had to live."

Propensity - *Bent, disposition*
Wight - *A human being*
Tarried - *To remain stay*
Lank - *Learn, thin*
Eloped - *To run off secretly*
Appalling - *Causing dismay*
Chastisement - *Rebuke*

When school hours were over, Ichabod was even the companion and playmate of the larger boys; and on holiday afternoons would convoy some of the smaller ones home, who happened to have pretty sisters, or good housewives for mothers, noted for the comforts of the cupboard. Indeed it behooved him to keep on good terms with his pupils. The revenue arising from his school would have been scarcely sufficient to furnish him with daily bread, for he was a huge feeder and, though lank, had the *dilating* powers of an anaconda. To help out his maintenance he was, according to custom in those parts, boarded and lodged at the homes of his pupils a week at a time; thus going the rounds of the neighborhood, with all his worldly effects tied up in a cotton handkerchief.

That this might not be too *onerous* for his rustic patrons, he assisted the farmers occasionally by helping to make hay, mending the fences, and driving the cows from pasture. He laid aside, too, all the dominant dignity with which he lorded it in the school, and became wonderfully gentle and ingratiating. He found favour in the eyes of the mothers by petting the children, particularly the youngest, and he would sit with a child on one knee, and rock a cradle with his foot for whole hours together.

In addition to his other vocations, he was the singing master of the neighborhood, and picked up many bright shillings by instructing the young folks in psalmody. Thus, by divers little makeshifts, the worthy pedagogue got on tolerably enough and was thought, by all who understood nothing of the labor of headwork, to have a wonderfully easy life of it.

The schoolmaster is generally a man of some importance in the female circle of a rural neighborhood, being considered a kind of idle, gentlemanlike personage, of vastly superior taste and accomplishments to the rough country swains. How he would figure among the country *damsels* in the churchyard, between services on Sundays! - gathering grapes for them from the wild vines that overran the surrounding trees; reciting for their amusement all the *epitaphs* on the tombstones; while the more bashful *bumpkins* hung sheepishly back, envying his superior elegance and address.

He was, moreover, esteemed by the women as a man of great erudition, for he had read several books quite through,

Dilating - *To make wider*
Onerous - *Burdensome*
Damsels - *A young on a tomb*
Epitaphs - *A poem*
Bumpkins - *A simple rustic, poor village man*
Direful - *Awful, terrible*

and was a perfect master of Cotton Mather's 'History of New England Witchcraft'. His appetite for the marvelous was extraordinary. It was often his delight, after his school was dismissed, to stretch himself on the clover bordering the little brook and there con over old Mather's *direful* tales in the gathering dusk.

Then, as he *wended* his way to the farmhouse where he happened to be quartered, every sound of nature, the boding cry of the tree toad, the *dreary hooting* of the screech owl, fluttered his excited imagination. His only resource on such occasions was to sing psalm tunes; and the good people of Sleepy Hollow were often filled with awe at hearing his nasal melody floating along the dusky road.

Another of his sources of fearful pleasure was to pass long winter evenings with the old Dutch wives, as they sat spinning by the fire, with a row of apples roasting and spluttering along the hearth, and listen to their marvelous tales of ghosts and goblins, haunted bridges and haunted houses, and particularly of the headless horseman. But if there was a pleasure in all this while snugly cuddling in the chimney corner, it was dearly purchased by the terrors of his subsequent walk homeward. How often did he shrink with *curdling* awe at some rushing blast, howling among the trees of a snowy night, in the idea that it was the Galloping Hessian of the Hollow!

All these, however, were mere phantoms of the dark. Daylight put mend to all these evils. He would have passed a pleasant life of it if his path had not been crossed by a being that causes more *perplexity* to mortal man than ghosts, goblins, and the whole race of witches put together, and that was -- a woman.

Among the musical disciples who assembled, one evening in each week, to receive his instructions in psalmody was Katrina Van Tassel, the only child of a substantial Dutch farmer. She was a blooming *lass* of fresh eighteen, plump as a partridge, ripe and melting and rosy-cheeked as one of her father's peaches, and universally famed, not merely for her beauty, but her vast expectations. She was withal a little of a coquette, as might be perceived in her dress. She wore ornaments of pure yellow gold to set off her charms, and a provokingly short petticoat to display the prettiest foot and ankle in the country round.

Wended - *To proceed/go*
Dreary - *Dull, boring*
Curdling - *To spoil*
Lass - *A girl or young woman*

Ichabod Crane had a soft and foolish heart toward, the sex; and it is not to be wondered at that so tempting a morsel soon found favour in his eyes, more especially after he had visited her in her paternal **mansion**. Old Baltus Van Tassel was a perfect picture of a thriving, contented, liberal-hearted farmer. He seldom, it is true, sent either his eyes or his thoughts beyond the boundaries of his own farm; but within those everything was snug, happy, and abundant.

The Van Tassel ***stronghold*** was situated on the banks of the Hudson, in one of those green, sheltered, fertile nooks in which the Dutch farmers are so fond of nestling. A great elm tree spread its broad branches over it, at the foot of which bubbled up a spring of the softest and sweetest water. Hard by the farmhouse was a vast ***barn***, every window and crevice of which seemed bursting forth with the treasures of the farm. Rows of pigeons were enjoying the sunshine on the roof. Sleek unwieldy porkers were grunting in the repose and abundance of their pens. A stately ***squadron*** of snowy geese were riding in an adjoining pond, convoying whole fleets of ducks; regiments of turkeys were ***gobbling*** through the farmyard.

The ***pedagogue's*** mouth watered as he looked upon this ***sumptuous*** promise of luxurious winter fare. In his devouring mind's eye he pictured to himself every roasting pig running about with an apple in his mouth; the pigeons were ***snugly*** put to bed in a comfortable pie, and tucked in with a ***coverlet*** of crust.

As the enraptured Ichabod fancied all this, and as he rolled his great green eyes over the fat meadowlands, the rich fields of wheat, rye, buckwheat, and Indian corn, and the orchard, burdened with ruddy fruit, which surrounded the warm tenement of Van Tassel, his heart yearned after the damsel who was to inherit these domains, and his imagination expanded with the idea how they might be readily turned into cash, and the money invested in immense tracts of wild land, and shingle palaces in the ***wilderness***. His busy fancy already presented to him the blooming Katrina, with a whole family of children, mounted on the top of a wagon loaded with household ***trumpery***; and he beheld himself bestriding a pacing mare, with a colt at her heels, setting out for Kentucky, Tennessee, or the Lord knows where.

Resplendent - *Shining brilliantly*
Trumpery - *Rubbish, trash*
Stronghold - *A well-fortified place*
Barn - *A building for storing hay, grain, etc.*
Gobbling - *To swallow or eat hastily*

When he entered the house, the conquest of his heart was complete. It was one of those spacious farmhouses, with high-ridged but low-sloping roofs, built in the style handed down from the first Dutch settlers, the projecting *eaves* forming a *piazza* along the front. From the piazza the wondering Ichabod entered the hall, which formed the center of the mansion. Here, rows of ***resplendent pewter***, ranged on a long dresser, dazzled his eyes.

In one corner stood a huge bag of wool ready to be spun; ears of Indian corn and strings of dried apples and peaches hung in gay *festoons* along the walls; and a door left ajar gave him a peep into the best *parlour*, where the claw-footed chairs and dark mahogany tables shone like mirrors. Mock oranges and conch shells decorated the mantelpiece; strings of various colored birds' eggs were suspended above it, and a corner cupboard, knowingly left open, displayed immense treasures of old silver and well-mended china.

From the moment Ichabod laid his eyes upon these regions of delight, the peace of his mind was at an end, and his only study was how to win the heart of the peerless daughter of Van Tassel. In this enterprise, however, he had to encounter a host of rustic admirers, who kept a watchful and angry eye upon each other, but were ready to fly out in the common cause against any new competitor. Among these the most *formidable* was a burly, roaring, roistering blade of the name of Brom Van Brunt, the hero of the country round, which rang with his feats of strength and hardihood.

He was broad-shouldered, with short curly black hair, and a bluff but not unpleasant countenance, having a ***mingled*** air of fun and arrogance. From his Herculean frame, he had received the nickname of "Brom Bones." He was famed for great skill in horsemanship; he was foremost at all races and cockfights; and, with the ***ascendancy*** which bodily strength acquires in rustic life, was the umpire in all disputes.

He was always ready for either a fight or a frolic, but had more mischief and good humor than ill will in his composition. He had three or four boon companions who regarded him as their model, and at the head of whom he scoured the country, attending every scene of *feud* or merriment for

Festoons - *A string or chain of flowers*
Parlour - *A living room*
Feud - *A bitter quarrel*
Gallantries - *A courageous action*

miles round. Sometimes his crew would be heard dashing along past the farmhouses at midnight, with **whoop** and **halloo**, and the old dames would exclaim, "Aye, there goes Brom Bones and his gang!"

This hero had for some time singled out the blooming Katrina for the object of his uncouth **gallantries**; and though his amorous toyings were something like the gentle caresses of a bear, yet it was whispered that she did not altogether discourage his hopes. Certain it is, his advances were signals for rival candidates to retire; in so much that, when his horse was seen tied to Van Tassel's paling on a Sunday night, all other suitors passed by in despair.

Such was the formidable rival with whom Ichabod Crane had to contend. Considering all things, a stouter man than he would have shrunk from the competition. Ichabod had, however, a happy mixture of *pliability* and perseverance in his nature; he was in form and spirit like a *supplejack* - though he bent, he never broke.

To have taken the field openly against his rival would have been madness. Ichabod, therefore, made his advances in a quiet and gently *insinuating* manner. Under cover of his character of singing master, he had made frequent visits at the farmhouse, carrying on his suit with the daughter by the side of the spring under the great elm, while Balt Van Tassel sat smoking his evening pipe at one end of the piazza and his little wife plied her spinning wheel at the other.

I profess not to know how women's hearts are wooed and won. To me they have always been matters of riddle and admiration. But certain it is that from the moment Ichabod Crane made his advances, the interests of Brom Bones declined; his horse was no longer seen tied at the paiings on Sunday nights, and a deadly feud gradually arose between him and the schoolmaster of Sleepy Hollow. Brom would fain have carried matters to open warfare, and Ichabod had overheard a boast by Bones that he would "double the schoolmaster up, and lay him on a shelf of his own schoolhouse"; but Ichabod was too wary to give him an opportunity.

Brom had no alternative but to play off boorish practical jokes upon his rival. Bones and his gang of rough riders smoked out Ichabod's singing school by stopping up the

Pliability - *Flexible*
Supplejack - *A strong cane*
Insinuating - *Tending to instill doubts*
Psalmody - *The art of setting psalms to music*
Pensive - *Thoughtful*
Ragged - *Clothed in torn garments*

chimney; broke into the schoolhouse at night and turned everything **topsy-turvy**. But what was still more annoying, Brom took opportunities of turning him to ridicule in presence of his mistress, and had a scoundrel dog whom he taught to whine in the most ludicrous manner, and introduced as a rival of Ichabod's to instruct Katrina in **psalmody**.

In this way matters went on for some time. On a fine autumn afternoon, Ichabod, in **pensive** mood, sat enthroned on the lofty stool whence he usually watched all the concerns of his little schoolroom. His scholars were all busily intent upon their books, or slyly whispering behind them with one eye kept upon the master; and a kind of buzzing stillness reigned. It was suddenly interrupted by the appearance of a Negro, mounted on the back of a **ragged** colt. He came clattering up to the school door with an invitation to Ichabod to attend a merrymaking to be held that evening at Mynheer Van Tassel's.

All was now bustle and hubbub in the lately quiet schoolroom. The scholars were hurried through their lessons, without stopping at trifles; those who were tardy had a smart application now and then in the rear to quicken their speed, and the whole school was turned loose an hour before the usual time.

The **gallant** Ichabod now spent at least an extra half hour at his toilet, brushing and **furbishing** up his only suit, of rusty black. That he might make his appearance in the true style of a cavalier, he borrowed a horse from the farmer with whom he was staying. The animal was a broken-down plow horse that had outlived almost everything but his **viciousness**.

He was **gaunt** and **shaggy**, with a ewe neck and a head like a hammer; his rusty mane and tail were tangled and knotted with burrs; one eye had lost its pupil, and was glaring and spectral, but the other had the gleam of a genuine devil. In his day he must have had fire and **mettle**, if we may judge from the name he bore of Gunpowder.

Ichabod was a suitable figure for such a steed. He rode with short stirrups, which brought his knees nearly up to the **pommel** of the saddle; his sharp elbows stuck out like grasshoppers'; he carried his whip perpendicularly in his hand, like a scepter, and, as his horse jogged on, the motion of his

Furbishing - *To polish*
Gaunt - *Very thin*
Shaggy - *Covered with long rough hair*
Mettle - *Saltier*
Pommel - *A knob*
Garnished - *That adds flavour*
Dimpled - *A small dent on the face*

arms was not unlike the flapping of a pair of wings. A small wool hat rested nearly on the top of his nose, and the skirts of his black coat fluttered out almost to the horse's tail.

Around him nature wore that rich and golden livery which we always associate with the idea of abundance. As he jogged slowly on his way, his eye ranged with delight over the treasures of jolly autumn. On all sides he beheld vast stores of apples gathered into baskets and barrels for the market, others heaped up in rich piles for the cider press.

Farther on he beheld great fields of Indian corn, and the yellow pumpkins lying beneath them, turning up their fair round bellies to the sun. He passed the fragrant buckwheat fields, and as he beheld them, soft anticipations stole over his mind of dainty slapjacks, well buttered and **garnished** with honey by the delicate little **dimpled** hand of Katrina Van Tassel. It was toward evening that Ichabod arrived at the castle of the Eleer Van Tassel, which he found **thronged** with the pride and flower of the adjacent country. Old farmers, a spare leathern-faced race, in homespun coats and breeches, blue stockings, huge shoes, and magnificent pewter buckles. Their brisk withered little dames, in close crimped caps, long-waisted short gowns, homespun **petticoats**, and gay calico pockets hanging on the outside. Buxom lasses, almost as **antiquated** in dress as their mothers, excepting where a straw hat, a fine ribbon, or perhaps a white frock gave symptoms of city innovation.

The sons, in short square-skirted coats with rows of stupendous brass buttons, and their hair generally queued with an eelskin in the fashion of the times, eelskins being esteemed as a potent nourisher and strengthener of the hair. Brom Bones, however, was the hero of the scene, having come to the gathering on his favorite steed, Daredevil, a creature, like himself, full of **mettle** and mischief, and which no one but himself could manage.

Ichabod was a kind and thankful creature, whose spirits rose with eating as some men do with drink. He could not help rolling his large eyes round him on the ample charms of a genuine Dutch country tea table in the **sumptuous** time of autumn. Such heaped-up platters of cakes and crullers of various kinds, known only to experienced Dutch housewives!

Petticoats - *An underskirts*
Antiquated - *Adhering to the past*
Mettle - *Courage*
Sumptuous - *Luxurious*

And then there were apple pies and peach pies and pumpkin pies, besides slices of ham and smoked beef; and, moreover, delectable dishes of preserved plums, and peaches, and pears, and *quinces*, not to mention broiled shad and roasted chickens; together with bowls of milk and cream, with the motherly teapot sending up its clouds of vapor from the midst.

Ichabod chuckled with the possibility that he might one day be lord of all this scene of almost unimaginable luxury and splendor. Then, he thought, how soon he'd turn his back upon the old schoolhouse and snap his fingers in the face of every niggardly patron!

And now the sound of the music from the hall summoned to the dance. The musician was an old gray-headed Negro, who had been the itinerant orchestra of the neighborhood for more than half a century. His instrument was as old and battered as himself. He accompanied every movement of the bow with a motion of the head, bowing almost to the ground and stamping with his foot whenever a fresh couple were to start.

Ichabod prided himself upon his dancing as much as upon his vocal powers. Not a limb, not a fiber about him was idle as his loosely hung frame in full motion went *clattering* about the room. How could the flogger of urchins be otherwise than animated and joyous! The lady of his heart was his partner in the dance, and smiling graciously in reply to all his *amorous oglings*; while Brom Bones, sorely smitten with love and jealousy, sat brooding by himself in one corner.

When the dance was at an end, Ichabod was attracted to a knot of the sager folks, who, with old Van Tassel, sat smoking at one end of the piazza, gossiping over former times, and drawing out long stories about ghosts and apparitions, mourning cries and *wailings*, seen and heard in the neighborhood. Some mention was made of the woman in white, who haunted the dark glen at Raven Rock, and was often heard to shriek on winter nights before a storm, having perished there in the snow.

The chief part of the stories, however, turned upon the favourite specter of Sleepy Hollow, the Headless Horseman, who had been heard several times of late near the bridge that crossed the brook in the woody dell next to the church; and, it

Amorous - *Inclined to love*
Oglings - *To look*
Wailings - *Loud cries*
Spectre - *A ghost*
Affirmed - *Confirmed*
Lingered - *To remain or stay on*

was said, tethered his horse nightly among the graves in the churchyard.

The tale was told of old Brouwer, a most **heretical** disbeliever in ghosts, how he met the horseman returning from his foray into Sleepy Hollow, and was obliged to get up behind him; how they galloped over hill and swamp until they reached the church bridge. There the horseman suddenly turned into a skeleton, threw old Brouwer into the brook, and sprang away over the treetops with a clap of thunder.

This story was matched by Brom Bones, who made light of the Galloping Hessian as an arrant jockey. He *affirmed* that, on returning one night from a neighbouring village, he had been overtaken by this midnight trooper; that he had offered to race with him for a bowl of punch, and should have won it, too; but just as they came to the church bridge, the Hessian bolted, and vanished in a flash of fire.

The revel now gradually broke up. The old farmers gathered together their families in their wagons, and were heard for some time rattling along over the distant hills. Some of the damsels mounted behind their favorite swains, and their lighthearted laughter, *mingling* with the clatter of hoofs, echoed along the silent woodlands.

Ichabod only *lingered* behind, according to the custom of country lovers, to have a tete-a-tete with the heiress, fully convinced that he was now on the highroad to success. Something, however, I fear me, must have gone wrong, for he *sallied forth*, after no very great interval, with an air quite *desolate* and *chopfallen*. Oh, these women! these women! Was Katrina's encouragement of the poor *pedagogue* all a mere trick to secure her conquest of his rival! Let it suffice to say, Ichabod stole forth with the air of one who had been sacking a *henroost*, rather than a fair lady's heart. Without looking to the right or left, he went straight to the stable, and with several hearty cuffs and kicks, roused his steed most uncourteously.

It was the very witching time of night that Ichabod, heavyhearted and crestfallen, pursued his travel homeward. Far below, the Tappan Zee spread its dusky waters. In the dead hush of midnight he could hear the faint barking of a watchdog from the opposite shore. The night grew darker and darker; the stars seemed to sink deeper in the sky, and driving

---

Sallied - *A sudden rushing forth*
Desolate - *Barren, deprived*
Chopfallen - *Dejected*
Pedagogue - *A school teacher*
Henroost - *A place where hens lay eggs*
Goblins - *The name of a spirit*

clouds occasionally hid them from his sight. He had never felt so lonely and dismal.

All the stories of ghosts and **goblins** that he had heard earlier now came crowding upon his recollection. He would, moreover, soon be approaching the very place where many of the scenes of the ghost stories had been laid.

Just ahead, where a small brook crossed the road, a few rough logs lying side by side served for a bridge. A group of oaks and chestnuts, matted thick with wild grapevines, threw a cavernous gloom over it. Ichabod gave Gunpowder half a score of kicks in his starvelling ribs, and attempted to dash briskly across the bridge; but instead of starting forward, the perverse old animal only plunged to the opposite side of the road into a thicket of brambles.

He came to a stand just by the bridge, with a suddenness that nearly sent his rider sprawling over his head. Just at this moment, in the dark shadow on the margin of the brook, Ichabod beheld something huge, misshapen, black, and towering. It stirred not, but seemed gathered up in the gloom, like some gigantic monster ready to spring upon the traveller.

The hair of the affrighted schoolteacher rose upon his head, but, summoning up a show of courage, he demanded in stammering accents, "Who are you!" He received no reply. He repeated his demand in a still more agitated voice. Still there was no answer. Once more he *cudgeled* the sides of the inflexible Gunpowder and, shutting his eyes, broke forth with involuntary fervor into a psalm tune. Just then the shadowy object of alarm put itself in motion and, with a scramble and a bound, stood at once in the middle of the road. He appeared to be a horseman of large **dimensions**, and mounted on a black horse of powerful frame. He kept aloof on one side of the road, jogging along on the blind side of old Gunpowder, who had now got over his waywardness.

Ichabod quickened his steed, in hopes of leaving this midnight companion behind. The stranger, however, quickened his horse to an equal pace. Ichabod pulled up, and fell into a walk, thinking to lag behind - the other did the same. His heart began to sink within him. There was something in the stranger's moody silence that was ***appalling***.

Desperation - *Reckless ness*
Knoll - *A small rounded hill*
Girths - *The measure around any thing*
Clasping - *A firm, grip*
Jolted - *To knock sharply*
Cleave - *To remain faithful*

It was soon fearfully accounted for. On mounting a rising ground, which brought the figure of his fellow traveler in relief against the sky, gigantic in height, and *muffled* in a cloak, Ichabod was *horrorstruck* on *perceiving* that he was headless! But his horror was still more increased on observing that the stranger's head was carried before him on the pommel of the saddle.

Ichabod's terror rose to *desperation*; he rained a shower of kicks and blows upon Gunpowder, hoping to give his companion the slip, but the specter started full jump with him. Away then they dashed, stones flying and sparks flashing at every bound. Ichabod's flimsy garments fluttered in the air, as he stretched his long lank body away over his horse's head in the eagerness of his flight.

They had now reached that stretch of the road which descends to Sleepy Hollow, shaded by trees for about a quarter of a mile, where it crosses the famous church bridge just before the green *knoll* on which stands the church.

Gunpowder, who seemed possessed with a demon, plunged headlong downhill. As yet his panic had given his unskillful rider an apparent advantage in the chase; but just as he had got halfway through the hollow, the *girths* of the saddle gave way, and Ichabod felt it slipping from under him. He had just time to save himself by *clasping* old Gunpowder round the neck when the saddle fell to the earth. He had much ado to maintain his seat, sometimes slipping on one side, sometimes on another, and sometimes *jolted* on the high ridge of his horse's backbone, with a violence that he feared would *cleave* him *asunder*.

An opening in the trees now cheered him with the hopes that the church bridge was at hand. He saw the whitewashed walls of the church dimly glaring under the trees beyond. He recollected the place where Brom Bones's ghostly competitor had disappeared. "If I can but reach that bridge," thought Ichabod, "I am safe." Just then he heard the black steed *panting* and blowing close behind him; he even fancied that he felt his hot breath.

Another convuisive kick in the ribs, and old Gunpowder sprang upon the bridge; he thundered over the *resounding* planks; he gained the opposite side; and now Ichabod cast

Panting - *Breathing hard and quickly*
Resounding - *Making an echoing sound*
Brimstone - *An obsolete name for sulphur*
Dodge - *To elude*
Steed - *A high-spirited*

a look behind to see if his pursuer should vanish, according to rule, in a flash of fire and *brimstone*. Just then he saw the goblin rising in his stirrups, in the very act of *hurling* his head at him. Ichabod endeavored to *dodge* the horrible *missile*, but too late. It encountered his cranium with a tremendous crash - he was tumbled headlong into the dust, and Gunpowder, the black *steed*, and the goblin rider passed by like a whirlwind.

The next morning old Gunpowder was found without his saddle, and with the bridle under his feet, soberly cropping the grass at his master's gate. Ichabod did not make his appearance at breakfast; dinner hour came, but no Ichabod. The boys assembled at the schoolhouse, and strolled idly about the banks of the brook; but no schoolmaster.

An inquiry was set on foot, and after *diligent* investigation they came upon the saddle *trampled* in the dirt. The tracks of horses' hoofs deeply dented in the road were traced to the bridge, beyond which, on the bank of a broad part of the brook, was found the hat of the unfortunate Ichabod, and close beside it a shattered pumpkin. The brook was searched, but the body of the schoolmaster was not to be discovered.

The mysterious event caused much *speculation* at the church on the following Sunday. Knots of gazers were collected in the churchyard, at the bridge, and at the spot where the hat and pumpkin had been found. They shook their heads, and came to the conclusion that Ichabod had been carried off by the Galloping Hessian. As he was a bachelor, and in nobody's debt, nobody troubled his head anymore about him.

It is true, an old farmer who had been down to New York on a visit several years after brought home the intelligence that Ichabod Crane was still alive; that he had only changed his quarters to a distant part of the country, had kept school and studied law at the same time, had turned politician, and finally had been made a justice of the Ten Pound Court. Brom Bones too, who shortly after his rival's disappearance conducted the blooming Katrina to the altar, was observed to look exceedingly knowing whenever the story of Ichabod was related, and always burst into a hearty laugh at the mention of the pumpkin, which led some to suspect that he knew more about the matter than he chose to tell.

Supernatural - *Divine*
Loitering - *To move about aimlessly*
Melancholy - *Sadness*
Psalm - *A sacred song*
Solitudes - *Seclusion, lonely place*

The old country wives, however, who are the best judges of these matters, maintain to this day that Ichabod was spirited away by **supernatural** means. The bridge became more than ever an object of **superstitious awe**, and that may be the reason why the road has been altered of late years, so as to approach the church by the border of the millpond.

The schoolhouse, being deserted, soon fell to decay, and was reported to be haunted by the the ghost of the unfortunate teacher; and the plowboy, **loitering** homeward of a still summer evening, has often fancied Ichabod's voice at a distance, chanting a **melancholy psalm** tune among the tranquil **solitudes** of Sleepy Hollow.

Food For Thought

Allthough the nature of the ghost, a Headless Horseman is left open for interpretation of the readers, the story implies that the ghost was none other than Brom Bones in disguise to remove Ichabod Crane from his path and marry the wealthy Katrina. But what do the old Dutch wives of the countryside still believe? Do you believe that spirits and ghosts exist?

An Understanding

Q. 1. Where is the story from? What is the 'Sleepy Hollow' and what is it renowned for?
Ans. _____

Q. 2. What is the legend of the 'Sleepy Hollow' all about? Describe the story briefly.
Ans. _____

Q. 3. Who was Ichabod Crane, and how did he disappear?
Ans. _____

Q. 4. Who is Brom Bones and what does he do to marry Katrina Van Tassel, the daughter and the sole child of the wealthy farmer, Baltus Van Tassel?
Ans. _____

A Matter Of Sentiment
– Saki

IT 'was the eve of the great race, and scarcely a member of Lady Susan's house-party had as yet a single bet on. It was one of those unsatisfactory years when one horse held a commanding market position, not by reason of any general belief in its crushing *superiority*, but because it was extremely difficult to pitch on any other candidate to whom to pin ones faith. Peradventure II was the favourite, not in the sense of being a popular fancy, but by virtue of a lack of confidence in any one of his rather undistinguished rivals. The brains of club-land were much exercised in seeking out possible merit where none was very obvious to the naked intelligence, and the house-party at Lady Susan's was possessed by the same uncertainty and *irresolution* that infected wider circles.

"It is just the time for bringing off a good coup," said Bertie van Tahn.

"Undoubtedly. But with what?" demanded Clovis for the twentieth time.

The women of the party were just as keenly interested in the matter, and just as helplessly perplexed; even the mother of Clovis, who usually got good racing information from her dressmaker, confessed herself fancy free on this occasion. Colonel Drake, who was professor of military history at a minor *cramming* establishment, was the only person who had a definite selection for the event, but as his choice varied every three hours he was worse than useless as an inspired guide. The crowning difficulty of the problem was that it could only be fitfully and *furtively* discussed. Lady Susan disapproved of racing. She disapproved of many things; some people went as far as to say that she disapproved of most things. Disapproval was to her what *neuralgia* and fancy needlework are to many other women. She disapproved of early morning tea and auction bridge, of skiing and the two-step, of the Russian ballet and the Chelsea Arts Club ball, of the French policy in Morocco and the British policy everywhere. It was not that she was particularly strict or narrow in her views of life, but she had been the eldest sister of a large family of self-indulgent children, and her particular form of *indulgence* had consisted in openly disapproving of the foibles of the

Superiority - *Greater in quality*
Irresolution - *Hesitation*
Cramming - *To memorise information*
Furtively - *Sly and secretive*
Neuralgia - *Sharp, severe never pain*

others. Unfortunately the hobby had grown up with her. As she was rich, **influential**, and very, very kind, most people were content to count their early tea as well lost on her behalf. Still, the necessity for hurriedly dropping the discussion of an **enthralling** topic, and suppressing all mention of it during her presence on the scene, was an **affliction** at a moment like the present, when time was slipping away and indecision was the prevailing note.

After a lunch-time of rather strangled and uneasy conversation, Clovis managed to get most of the party together at the further end of the kitchen gardens, on the pretext of admiring the Himalayan **pheasants**. He had made an important discovery. Motkin, the butler, who (as Clovis expressed it) had grown prematurely grey in Lady Susan's service, added to his other excellent qualities an intelligent interest in matters connected with the Turf. On the subject of the forthcoming race he was not illuminating, except in so far that he shared the prevailing unwillingness to see a winner in Peradventure II. But where he **outshone** all the members of the house-party was in the fact that he had a second cousin who was head stable-lad at a neighbouring racing establishment, and usually gifted with much inside information as to private form and possibilities. Only the fact of her ladyship having taken it into her head to invite a house-party for the last week of May had prevented Mr. Motkin from paying a visit of consultation to his relative with respect to the big race; there was still time to cycle over if he could get leave of absence for the afternoon on some **specious** excuse.

"Let's jolly well hope he does," said Bertie van Tahn; "under the circumstances a second cousin is almost as useful as second sight."

"That stable ought to know something, if knowledge is to be found anywhere," said Mrs. Packletide hopefully.

"I expect you'll find he'll echo my fancy for Motorboat," said Colonel Drake.

At this moment the subject had to be hastily dropped. Lady Susan bore down upon them, leaning on the arm of Clovis's mother, to whom she was **confiding** the fact that she disapproved of the craze for Pekingese **spaniels**. It was the third thing she had found time to disapprove of since lunch, without counting her silent and permanent disapproval of the way Clovis's mother did her hair.

"We have been admiring the Himalayan pheasants," said Mrs. Packletide **suavely**.

Influential - *Well-known*
Enthralling - *Captivating*
Affliction - *A condition of great distreass*
Pheasants - *A variety of long-tailed*
Outshone - *To shine more brightly*
Spaniels - *Submissive persons*

"They went off to a bird-show at Nottingham early this morning," said Lady Susan, with the air of one who disapproves of hasty and ill-considered lying.

"Their house, I mean; such perfect *roosting* arrangements, and all so clean," resumed Mrs. Packletide, with an increased glow of enthusiasm. The odious Bertie van Tahn was murmuring audible prayers for Mrs. Packletide's ultimate *estrangement* from the paths of falsehood.

"I hope you don't mind dinner being a quarter of an hour late tonight," said Lady Susan; "Motkin has had an urgent *summons* to go and see a sick relative this afternoon. He wanted to bicycle there, but I am sending him in the motor."

"How very kind of you! Of course we don't mind dinner being put off." The assurances came with *unanimous* and hearty sincerity.

At the dinner-table that night an undercurrent of furtive curiosity directed itself towards Motkin's *impassive countenance*. One or two of the guests almost expected to find a slip of paper concealed in their napkins, bearing the name of the second cousin's selection. They had not long to wait. As the butler went round with the murmured question, "Sherry?" he added in an even lower tone the cryptic words, "Better not." Mrs. Packletide gave a start of alarm, and refused the sherry; there seemed some sinister suggestion in the butler's warning, as though her hostess had suddenly become addicted to the Borgia habit. A moment later the explanation flashed on her that "Better Not" was the name of one of the runners in the big race. Clovis was already pencilling it on his cuff, and Colonel Drake, in his turn, was signalling to every one in hoarse whispers and dumb-show the fact that he had all along fancied "B.N."

Early next morning a *sheaf* of telegrams went Townward, representing the market commands of the house-party and servants' hall.

It was a wet afternoon, and most of Lady Susan's guests hung about the hall, waiting apparently for the appearance of tea, though it was scarcely yet due. The advent of a telegram quickened every one into a flutter of expectancy; the page who brought the telegram to Clovis waited with unusual alertness to know if there might be an answer.

Clovis read the message and gave an exclamation of annoyance.

Hoosting - *Percking*
Estrangement - *To turn away in feedings*
Summons - *A request command*
Unanimous - *Of one mind*
Sheaf - *Any bundle, cluster collection persons*

"No bad news, I hope," said Lady Susan. Every one else knew that the news was not good.

"It's only the result of the Derby," he blurted out; "Sadowa won; an utter outsider."

"Sadowa!" exclaimed Lady Susan; "you don't say so! How remarkable! It's the first time I've ever backed a horse; in fact I disapprove of horse-racing, but just for once in a way I put money on this horse, and it's gone and won."

"May I ask," said Mrs. Packletide, amid the general silence, "why you put your money on this particular horse? None of the sporting prophets mentioned it as having an outside chance."

"Well," said Lady Susan, "you may laugh at me, but it was the name that attracted me. You see, I was always mixed up with the Franco-German war; I was married on the day that the war was declared, and my eldest child was born the day that peace was signed, so anything connected with the war has always interested me. And when I saw there was a horse running in the Derby called after one of the battles in the Franco-German war, I said I *must* put some money on it, for once in a way, though I disapprove of racing. And it's actually won."

There was a general groan. No one groaned more deeply than the professor of military history.

Blurted - *To utter suddenly*
Disapprove - *To deplore, criticize*
Remarkable - *Worthy of notice*

Food For Thought

"Sadowa!" exclaimed Lady Susan, "You don't say so! How remarkable! It's the first time I've ever backed a horse." Why do you think Lady Susan betted on this horse when she disliked horse - racing? Does this justify the name of the story or you prefer to suggest something different? If 'Yes', name it and give reasons for your answer.

Greatest Humour Stories

An Understanding

Q. 1. Give a brief character sketch of Lady Susan. What were her likings and dislikings and why?
Ans. _____
_____
_____
_____
_____

Q. 2. What were the guests and members at Lady Susan's House - Party betting on? What was the eve all about?
Ans. _____
_____
_____
_____
_____

Q. 3. Name all the guests who attended Lady Susan's house - party?
Ans. _____
_____
_____
_____
_____

Q. 4. Who was Motkin and how was he a very important person in Lady Susan's household?
Ans. _____
_____
_____
_____
_____

The Princess And The Puma
~ O. Henry

There had to be a king and queen, of course. The king was a terrible old man who wore six-shooters and spurs, and shouted in such a tremendous voice that the rattlers on the prairie would run into their holes under the prickly pear. Before there was a royal family they called the man "Whispering Ben." When he came to own 50,000 acres of land and more cattle than he could count, they called him O'Donnell "the Cattle King."

The queen had been a Mexican girl from Laredo. She made a good, mild, Coloradoclaro wife, and even succeeded in teaching Ben to modify his voice sufficiently while in the house to keep the dishes from being broken. When Ben got to be king she would sit on the gallery of Espinosa Ranch and weave rush mats. When wealth became so irresistible and oppressive that **upholstered** chairs and a centre table were brought down from San Antone in the wagons, she bowed her smooth, dark head, and shared the fate of the Danaë.

To avoid *lèse-majesté* you have been presented first to the king and queen. They do not enter the story, which might be called "The Chronicle of the Princess, the Happy Thought, and the Lion that **Bungled** his Job."

Josefa O'Donnell was the surviving daughter, the princess. From her mother she inherited warmth of nature and a dusky, semi-tropic beauty. From Ben O'Donnell the royal she acquired a store in intrepidity, common sense, and the faculty of ruling. The combination was was worth going miles to see. Josefa while riding her pony at a gallop could put five out of six bullets through a tomato-can swinging at the end of a string. She could play for hours with a white kitten she owned, dressing it in all manner of absurd clothes. **Scorning** a pencil, she could tell you out of her head what 1545 two-year-olds would bring on the hoof, at $8.50 per head. Roughly speaking, the Espinosal Ranch is forty miles long and thirty broad - but mostly leased land. Josefa, on her pony, had prospected over every mile of it. Every **cow-puncher** on the range knew her by sight and was a loyal vassal. Ripley Givens, foreman of one of the Espinosal outfits, saw her one day, and made up his mind to form a royal matrimonial alliance. **Presumptuous**? No. In those days in the Nueces country a man was a man. And, after all, the title of cattle king does not **presuppose** blood royal.

Upholstered - *To furnish with curtains*
Bungled - *To work clumsily*
Scorning - *To regard with contempt*
Cow-puncher - *A cowboy*

Often it only signifies that its owner wears the crown in token of his magnificent qualities in the art of cattle stealing.

One day Ripley Givens rode over to the Double Elm Ranch to inquire about a bunch of strayed *yearlings*. He was late in setting out on his return trip, and it was sundown when he struck the White Horse Crossing of the Nueces. From there to his own camp it was sixteen miles. To the Espinosal ranchhouse it was twelve. Givens was tired. He decided to pass the night at the Crossing.

There was a fine water hole in the river-bed. The banks were thickly covered with great trees, undergrown with brush. Back from the water hole fifty yards was a stretch of curly mesquite grass - supper for his horse and bed for himself. Givens staked his horse, and spread out his saddle blankets to dry. He sat down with his back against a tree and rolled a cigarette. From somewhere in the dense timber along the river came a sudden, *rageful*, shivering wail. The pony danced at the end of his rope and blew a whistling snort of comprehending fear. Givens puffed at his cigarette, but he reached leisurely for his pistol-belt, which lay on the grass, and twirled the cylinder of his weapon tentatively. A great gar plunged with a loud splash into the water hole. A little brown rabbit skipped around a bunch of *catclaws* and sat twitching his whiskers and looking humorously at Givens. The pony went on eating grass.

It is well to be reasonably watchful when a Mexican lion sings *soprano* along the *arroyos* at sundown. The burden of his song may be that young calves and fat lambs are scarce, and that he has a carnivorous desire for your acquaintance.

In the grass lay an empty fruit can, cast there by some former sojourner. Givens caught sight of it with a grunt of satisfaction. In his coat pocket tied behind his saddle was a handful or two of ground coffee. Black coffee and cigarettes! What ranchero could desire more?

In two minutes he had a little fire going clearly. He started, with his can, for the water hole. When within fifteen yards of its edge he saw, between the bushes, a side-saddled pony with down-dropped reins cropping grass a little distance to his left. Just rising from her hands and knees on the brink of the water hole was Josefa O'Donnell. She had been drinking water, and she brushed the sand from the palms of her hands. Ten yards away, to her right, half concealed by a clump of *sacuista,* Givens saw the crouching form of the Mexican lion. His amber eyelids glared hungrily; six feet from them was the tip of the tail stretched straight, like a pointer's. His

Presumptuous - *Arrogant*
Presuppose - *To assume beforehand*
Yearlings - *Being a year old*
Rageful - *To act or speak with fury*
Catclaw - *Prickly plants*
Soprano - *The highest adult female voice*

hind-quarters rocked with the motion of the cat tribe preliminary to leaping.

Givens did what he could. His six-shooter was thirty-five yards away lying on the grass. He gave a loud yell, and dashed between the lion and the princess.

The "rucus," as Givens called it afterward, was brief and somewhat confused. When he arrived on the line of attack he saw a dim streak in the air, and heard a couple of faint cracks. Then a hundred pounds of Mexican lion plumped down upon his head and flattened him, with a heavy jar, to the ground. He remembered calling out: "Let up, now - no fair *gouging*!" and then he crawled from under the lion like a worm, with his mouth full of grass and dirt, and a big lump on the back of his head where it had struck the root of a water-elm. The lion lay motionless. Givens, feeling *aggrieved*, and suspicious of fouls, shook his fist at the lion, and shouted: "I'll rastle you again for twenty —" and then he got back to himself.

Josefa was standing in her tracks, quietly reloading her silver-mounted .38. It had not been a difficult shot. The lion's head made an easier mark than a tomato-can swinging at the end of a string. There was a provoking, teasing, maddening smile upon her mouth and in her dark eyes. The would-be-rescuing knight felt the fire of his fiasco burn down to his soul. Here had been his chance, the chance that he had dreamed of; and Momus, and not Cupid, had presided over it. The *satyrs* in the wood were, no doubt, holding their sides in hilarious, silent laughter. There had been something like vaudeville - say Signor Givens and his funny knockabout act with the stuffed lion.

"Is that you, Mr. Givens?" said Josefa, in her deliberate, saccharine contralto. "You nearly spoiled my shot when you yelled. Did you hurt your head when you fell?"

"Oh, no," said Givens, quietly; "that didn't hurt." He stooped *ignominiously* and dragged his best Stetson hat from under the beast. It was crushed and wrinkled to a fine comedy effect. Then he knelt down and softly stroked the fierce, open-jawed head of the dead lion.

"Poor old Bill!" he exclaimed, *mournfully*.

"What's that?" asked Josefa, sharply.

"Of course you didn't know, Miss Josefa," said Givens, with an air of one allowing *magnanimity* to triumph over grief. "Nobody can blame you. I tried to save him, but I couldn't let you know in time."

Gouging - *Swindling*
Aggrieved - *Offended*
Satyrs - *A class of woodland diets*
Ignominiously - *Disgraceful, shameful*

"Save who?"

"Why, Bill. I've been looking for him all day. You see, he's been our camp pet for two years. Poor old fellow, he wouldn't have hurt a cottontail rabbit. It'll break the boys all up when they hear about it. But you couldn't tell, of course, that Bill was just trying to play with you."

Josefa's black eyes burned steadily upon him. Ripley Givens met the test successfully. He stood rumpling the yellow-brown curls on his head **pensively**. In his eyes was regret, not unmingled with a gentle **reproach**. His smooth features were set to a pattern of indisputable sorrow. Josefa wavered.

"What was your pet doing here?" she asked, making a last stand. "There's no camp near the White Horse Crossing."

"The old rascal ran away from camp yesterday," answered Givens, readily. "It's a wonder the coyotes didn't scare him to death. You see, Jim Webster, our horse wrangler, brought a little terrier pup into camp last week. The pup made life miserable for Bill - he used to chase him around and chew his hind legs for hours at a time. Every night when bedtime came Bill would sneak under one of the boys' blankets and sleep to keep the pup from finding him. I reckon he must have been worried pretty desperate or he wouldn't have run away. He was always afraid to get out of sight of camp."

Josefa looked at the body of the fierce animal. Givens gently patted one of the formidable paws that could have killed a yearling calf with one blow. Slowly a red flush widened upon the dark olive face of the girl. Was it the signal of shame of the true sportsman who has brought down ignoble **quarry**? Her eyes grew softer, and the lowered lids drove away all their bright mockery.

"I'm very sorry," she said, humbly; "but he looked so big, and jumped so high that —"

"Poor old Bill was hungry," interrupted Givens, in quick defence of the deceased. "We always made him jump for his supper in camp. He would lie down and roll over for a piece of meat. When he saw you he thought he was going to get something to eat from you."

Suddenly Josefa's eyes opened wide.

"I might have shot you!" she exclaimed. "You ran right in between. You risked your life to save your pet! That was fine, Mr. Givens. I like a man who is kind to animals."

Mournfully - *Sorrowfully, gloomily*
Magnanimity - *Generosity*
Pensively - *Thoughtfully*
Reproach - *Blame, to find fault with*

Yes; there was even admiration in her gaze now. After all, there was a hero rising out of the ruins of the ***anti-climax.*** The look on Givens's face would have secured him a high position in the S.P.C.A.

"I always loved 'em," said he; "horses, dogs, Mexican lions, cows, alligators —"

"I hate alligators," instantly ***demurred*** Josefa; "crawly, muddy things!"

"Did I say alligators?" said Givens. "I meant antelopes, of course."

Josefa's conscience drove her to make further amends. She held out her hand ***penitently***. There was a bright, unshed drop in each of her eyes.

"Please forgive me, Mr. Givens, won't you? I'm only a girl, you know, and I was frightened at first. I'm very, very sorry I shot Bill. You don't know how ashamed I feel. I wouldn't have done it for anything."

Givens took the ***proffered*** hand. He held it for a time while he allowed the generosity of his nature to overcome his grief at the loss of Bill. At last it was clear that he had forgiven her.

"Please don't speak of it any more, Miss Josefa. 'Twas enough to frighten any young lady the way Bill looked. I'll explain it all right to the boys."

"Are you really sure you don't hate me?" Josefa came closer to him ***impulsively***. Her eyes were sweet - oh, sweet and pleading with gracious penitence. "I would hate any one who would kill my kitten. And how daring and kind of you to risk being shot when you tried to save him! How very few men would have done that!" Victory wrested from defeat! Vaudeville turned into drama! Bravo, Ripley Givens!

It was now twilight. Of course Miss Josefa could not be allowed to ride on to the ranch-house alone. Givens resaddled his pony in spite of that animal's ***reproachful*** glances, and rode with her. Side by side they galloped across the smooth grass, the princess and the man who was kind to animals. The prairie odours of fruitful earth and delicate bloom were thick and sweet around them. Coyotes ***yelping*** over there on the hill! No fear. And yet —

Josefa rode closer. A little hand seemed to grope. Givens found it with his own. The ponies kept an even ***gait***. The hands ***lingered*** together, and the owner of one explained.

Anti-climax - *An event, conclusion, statement, etc.*
Demurred - *To object*
Penitently - *Feeling sorrow*
Proffered - *Volunteered*
Impulsively - *Hasty, emotional decision*

Greatest Humour Stories

"I never was frightened before, but just think! How terrible it would be to meet a really wild lion! Poor Bill! I'm so glad you came with me!"

O'Donnell was sitting on the ranch gallery.

"Hello, Rip!" he shouted - "that you?"

"He rode in with me," said Josefa. "I lost my way and was late."

"Much obliged," called the cattle king. "Stop over, Rip, and ride to camp in the morning."

But Givens would not. He would push on to camp. There was a bunch of **steers** to start off on the trail at daybreak. He said goodnight, and trotted away.

An hour later, when the lights were out, Josefa, in her nightrobe, came to her door and called to the king in his own room across the brick-paved hallway:

"Say, Pop, you know that old Mexican lion they call the 'Gotch-eared Devil' - the one that killed Gonzales, Mr. Martin's sheep herder, and about fifty calves on the Salada range? Well, I settled his hash this afternoon over at the White Horse Crossing. Put two balls in his head with my .38 while he was on the jump. I knew him by the slice gone from his left ear that old Gonzales cut off with his **machete**. You couldn't have made a better shot yourself, Daddy."

"Bully for you!" thundered Whispering Ben from the darkness of the royal chamber.

Food For Thought

Why do you think that when Josefa shot the beast twice in its head, Ripley was stunned and he felt a bit foolish? Why did he concoct a story when he had literally risked his life by diving towards the lion bare-handed?

An Understanding

Q. 1. Who is Ben O'Donnell in the story and what is he known as? Describe the encounter between Ben O'Donnell's daughter, Josefa O'Donnell and Ripley Givens?
Ans. _____
_____
_____
_____
_____

Q. 2. Where did Ripley and Josefa meet? What happened during their first visit?
Ans. _____
_____
_____
_____
_____

Q. 3. Josefa knew that the Mexican Lion was the famous 'Gotech-eared Devil' as it was popularly called by the people. Then why did she believe in Ripley's story and held his hand in hers?
Ans. _____
_____
_____
_____
_____

Q. 4. Ripley's revolver was yards away at the campsite and the Mexican Lion was crouching just behind Josefa, his love. What did Ripley do to save her and what happened next?
Ans. _____
_____
_____
_____
_____

A Nose For The King
– Jack London

IN the morning calm of Korea, when its peace and *tranquillity* truly merited its ancient name, "Cho-sen," there lived a politician by name Yi Chin Ho. He was a man of parts, and--who shall say?--perhaps in no wise worse than politicians the world over. But, unlike his brethren in other lands, Yi Chin Ho was in jail. Not that he had *inadvertently* diverted to himself public moneys, but that he had inadvertently diverted too much. Excess is to be deplored in all things, even in grafting, and Yi Chin Ho's excess had brought him to most *deplorable straits.*

Ten thousand strings of cash he owed the government, and he lay in prison under sentence of death. There was one advantage to the situation--he had plenty of time in which to think. And he thought well. Then called he the jailer to him.

"Most worthy man, you see before you one most wretched," he began. "Yet all will be well with me if you will but let me go free for one short hour this night. And all will be well with you, for I shall see to your advancement through the years, and you shall come at length to the directorship of all the prisons of Cho-sen."

"How, now?" demanded the jailer. "What foolishness is this? One short hour, and you but waiting for your head to be chopped off! And I, with an aged and much-to-be-respected mother, not to say anything of a wife and several children of tender years! Out upon you for the scoundrel that you are!"

"From the Sacred City to the ends of all the Eight Coasts there is no place for me to hide," Yi Chin Ho made reply. "I am a man of wisdom, but of what worth my wisdom here in prison? Were I free, well I know I could seek out and obtain the money wherewith to repay the government. I know of a nose that will save me from all my difficulties."

"A nose!" cried the jailer.

"A nose," said Yi Chin Ho. "A remarkable nose, if I may say so, a most remarkable nose."

Tranquillity -
Calmness, peacefulness
Inadvertently -
Unintentional
Deplorable -
Lamentable, shameful
Straits - *Dilemma, plight*
Despairingly -
Hopelessly

The jailer threw up his hands *despairingly*. "Ah, what a wag you are, what a wag," he laughed. "To think that that very admirable wit of yours must go the way of the chopping-block!"

And so saying, he turned and went away. But in the end, being a man soft of head and heart, when the night was well along he permitted Yi Chin Ho to go.

Straight he went to the Governor, catching him alone and arousing him from his sleep.

"Yi Chin Ho, or I'm no Governor!" cried the Governor. "What do you here who should be in prison waiting on the chopping-block?"

"I pray your excellency to listen to me," said Yi Chin Ho, *squatting* on his hams by the bedside and lighting his pipe from the fire-box. "A dead man is without value. It is true, I am as a dead man, without value to the government, to your excellency, or to myself. But if, so to say, your excellency were to give me my freedom--"

"Impossible!" cried the Governor. "Besides, you are condemned to death."

"Your excellency well knows that if I can repay the ten thousand strings of cash, the government will pardon me,' Yi Chin Ho went on. "So, as I say, if your excellency were to give me my freedom for a few days, being a man of understanding, I should then repay the government and be in position to be of service to your excellency. I should be in position to be of very great service to your excellency."

"Have you a plan whereby you hope to obtain this money?" asked I the Governor.

"I have," said Yi Chin Ho.

"Then come with it to me to-morrow night; I would now sleep," said the Governor, taking up his snore where it had been interrupted.

On the following night, having again obtained leave of absence from the jailer, Yi Chin Ho presented himself at the Governor's bedside.

"Is it you, Yi Chin Ho?" asked the Governor. "And have you the plan ?"

"It is I, your excellency," answered Yi Chin Ho, "and the plan is here."

Squatting - *Crouching down as an animal*
Strings - *Slender cords*
Despairing - *Hopelessly*
Interrupted - *To cause or make a break in the continuity*

"Speak," commanded the Governor.

"The plan is here," repeated Yi Chin Ho, "here in my hand."

The Governor sat up and opened his eyes. Yi Chin Ho *proffered* in his hand a sheet of paper. The Governor held it to the light.

"Nothing but a nose," said he.

"A bit pinched, so, and so, your excellency," said Yi Chin Ho.

"Yes, a bit *pinched* here and there, as you say," said the Governor.

"*Withal* it is an exceeding corpulent nose, thus, and so, all in one place, at the end," proceeded Yi Chin Ho. "Your excellency would seek far and wide and many a day for that nose and find it not."

"An unusual nose," admitted the Governor.

"There is a wart upon it," said Yi Chin Ho.

"A most unusual nose," said the Governor. "Never have I seen the like. But what do you with this nose, Yi Chin Ho?"

"I seek it whereby to repay the money to the government," said Yi Chin Ho. "I seek it to be of service to your excellency, and I seek it to save my own worthless head. Further, I seek your excellency's seal upon this picture of the nose."

And the Governor laughed and affixed the seal of state, and Yi Chin Ho departed. For a month and a day he travelled the King's Road which leads to the shore of the Eastern Sea; and there, one night, at the gate of the largest *mansion* of a wealthy city he knocked loudly for admittance.

"None other than the master of the house will I see," said he fiercely to the frightened servants. "I travel upon the King's business."

Straightway was he led to an inner room, where the master of the house was roused from his sleep and brought *blinking* before him.

"You are Pak Chung Chang, head man of this city," said Yi Chin Ho in tones that were all-accusing. "I am upon the King's business."

Pinched - *To squeeze*
Withal - *In spite of all, besides, nevertheless*
Mansion - *A very large and impressive house*
Blinking - *Opening and closing the eye quickly*
Quavered - *To shake tremulously*

Greatest Humour Stories

Pak Chung Chang trembled. Well he knew the King's business was ever a terrible business. His knees smote together, and he near fell to the floor.

"The hour is late," he *quavered*. "Were it not well to--"

"The King's business never waits!" thundered Yi Chin Ho. "Come apart with me, and swiftly. I have an affair of moment to discuss with you.

"It is the King's affair," he added with even greater fierceness; so that Pak Chung Chang's silver pipe dropped from his nerveless fingers and *clattered* on the floor.

"Know then," said Yi Chin Ho, when they had gone apart, "that the King is troubled with an affliction, a very terrible *affliction*. In that he failed to cure, the Court physician has had nothing else than his head chopped off. From all the Eight Provinces have the physicians come to wait upon the King. Wise consultation have they held, and they have decided that for a remedy for the King's affliction nothing else is required than a nose, a certain kind of nose, a very peculiar certain kind of nose.

"Then by none other was I summoned than his excellency the prime minister himself. He put a paper into my hand. Upon this paper was the very peculiar kind of nose drawn by the physicians of the Eight Provinces, with the seal of state upon it.

"'Go,' said his excellency the prime minister. 'Seek out this nose, for the King's affliction is sore. And wheresoever you find this nose upon the face of a man, strike it off forthright and bring it in all haste to the Court, for the King must be cured. Go, and come not back until your search is rewarded.'

"And so I departed upon my quest," said Yi Chin Ho. "I have sought out the *remotest* corners of the kingdom; I have travelled the Eight Highways, searched the Eight Provinces, and sailed the seas of the Eight Coasts. And here I am."

With a great flourish he drew a paper from his girdle, unrolled it with many *snappings* and *cracklings*, and thrust it before the face of Pak Chung Chang. Upon the paper was the picture of the nose.

Pak Chung Chang stared upon it with *bulging* eyes.

"Never have I beheld such a nose," he began.

Affliction - *A state of pain, distress*
Remotest - *Secluded*
Snappings - *Breaking*
Cracklings - *The making of slight cracking sounds*
Dissemble - *To gived false*

Greatest Humour Stories

"There is a wart upon it," said Yi Chin Ho.

"Never have I beheld--" Pak Chung Chang began again.

"Bring your father before me," Yi Chin Ho interrupted sternly.

"My ancient and very-much-to-be-respected ancestor sleeps," said Pak Chung Chang.

"Why *dissemble*?" demanded Yi Chin Ho. "You know it is your father's nose. Bring him before me that I may strike it off and be gone. Hurry, lest I make bad report of you."

"Mercy!" cried Pak Chung Chang, falling on his knees. "It is impossible! It is impossible! You cannot strike off my father's nose. He cannot go down without his nose to the grave. He will become a laughter and a byword, and all my days and nights will be filled with woe. O reflect! Report that you have seen no such nose in your travels. You, too, have a father."

Pak Chung Chang *clasped* Yi Chin Ho's knees and fell to weeping on his sandals.

"My heart softens strangely at your tears," said Yi Chin Ho. "I, too, know *filial piety* and regard. But--" He hesitated, then added, as though thinking aloud, "It is as much as my head is worth."

"How much is your head worth?" asked Pak Chung Chang in a thin, small voice.

"A not remarkable head," said Yi Chin Ho. "An absurdly unremarkable head; but, such is my great foolishness, I value it at nothing less than one hundred thousand strings of cash."

"So be it," said Pak Chung Chang, rising to his feet.

"I shall need horses to carry the treasure," said Yi Chin Ho, "and men to guard it well as I journey through the mountains. There are robbers abroad in the land."

"There are robbers abroad in the land," said Pak Chung Chang, sadly. "But it shall be as you wish, so long as my ancient and very-much-to-be-respected ancestor's nose abide in its appointed place."

"Say nothing to any man of this occurrence," said Yi Chin Ho, "else will other and more loyal servants than I be sent to strike off your father's nose."

Clasped - *Firmly grasped*
Filial piety - *The important virtue*

And so Yi Chin Ho departed on his way through the mountains, blithe of heart and gay of song as he listened to the jingling bells of his treasure-laden ponies.

There is little more to tell. Yi Chin Ho prospered through the years. By his efforts the jailer attained at length to the directorship of all the prisons of Cho-sen; the Governor ultimately betook himself to the Sacred City to be prime minister to the King, while Yi Chin Ho became the King's boon companion and sat at table with him to the end of a round, fat life. But Pak Chung Chang fell into a melancholy, and ever after he shook his head sadly, with tears in his eyes, whenever he regarded the expensive nose of his ancient and very-much-to-be-respected ancestor.

Blithe - *Joyous, merry*
Jingling - *Tinkling*
Melancholy - *A gloomy state of mind*

Food For Thought

The Governor laughed at the most unusual nose drawn by Yi Chin Ho on a sheet of paper and affixed the seal of the state as urged by him. Do you think that this was the jackpot that Chin Ho Striked which finally changed his destiny? Give reasons for your answer.

An Understanding

Q. 1. Who was Yi Chin Ho and why was he in jail under the sentence of death?
Ans. _____
_____
_____
_____
_____

Q. 2. What was the ancient name of Korea and how did Yi Chin Ho address and persuade him to let him go free for an hour one night?
Ans. _____
_____
_____
_____
_____

Q. 3. What did Yi Chin Ho do after getting released from the prison? How did he influence the Governor and begged freedom for a few days?
Ans. _____
_____
_____
_____
_____

Q. 4. What was Yi Chin Ho's plan? How did he acquire the ten thousand strings of cash that he had embezzled as a public servant and repay the money to the Government?
Ans. _____
_____
_____
_____
_____

A Ramble In Aphasia
– O. Henry

MY wife and I parted on that morning in precisely our usual manner. She left her second cup of tea to follow me to the front door. There she plucked from my *lapel* the invisible strand of lint (the universal act of woman to proclaim ownership) and bade me to take care of my cold. I had no cold. Next came her kiss of parting - the lever kiss of domesticity flavored with Young Hyson. There was no fear of the *extemporaneous*, of variety spicing her infinite custom. With the deft touch of long *malpractice*, she dabbed awry my well-set scarf pin; and then, as I closed the door, I heard her morning slippers pattering back to her cooling tea.

When I set out I had no thought or premonition of what was to occur. The attack came suddenly. For many weeks I had been toiling, almost night and day, at a famous railroad law case that I won triumphantly but a few days previously. In fact, I had been digging away at the law almost without **cessation** for many years. Once or twice good Doctor Volney, my friend and physician, had warned me.

"If you don't slacken up, Belford," he said, "you'll go suddenly to pieces. Either your nerves or your brain will give way. Tell me, does a week pass in which you do not read in the papers of a case of ***aphasia*** - of some man lost, wandering nameless, with his past and his identity blotted out - and all from that little brain clot made by overwork or worry?"

"I always thought," said I, "that the clot in those instances was really to be found on the brains of the newspaper reporters."

Doctor Volney shook his head.

"The disease exists," he said. "You need a change or a rest. Court-room, office and home - there is the only route you travel. For recreation you - read law books. Better take warning in time."

"On Thursday nights," I said, defensively, "my wife and I play ***cribbage***. On Sundays she reads to me the weekly letter from her mother. That law books are not a recreation remains yet to be established."

Lapel - *The continuation of the turned*
Extemporaneous - *Spontaneous*
Malpractice - *Improper*
Aphasia - *Loss ability to speak*
Cribbage - *A card game for two*

Greatest Humour Stories

That morning as I walked I was thinking of Doctor Volney's words. I was feeling as well as I usually did - possibly in better spirits than usual.

I woke with stiff and cramped muscles from having slept long on the *incommodious* seat of a day coach. I leaned my head against the seat and tried to think. After a long time I said to myself: "I must have a name of some sort." I searched my pockets. Not a card; not a letter; not a paper or *monogram* could I find. But I found in my coat pocket nearly $3,000 in bills of large denomination. "I must be some one, of course," I repeated to myself, and began again to consider.

The car was well crowded with men, among whom, I told myself, there must have been some common interest, for they intermingled freely, and seemed in the best good humor and spirits. One of them - a stout, spectacled gentleman enveloped in a decided odor of *cinnamon* and aloes - took the vacant half of my seat with a friendly nod, and unfolded a newspaper. In the intervals between his periods of reading, we conversed, as travelers will, on current affairs. I found myself able to sustain the conversation on such subjects with credit, at least to my memory. By and by my companion said:

"You are one of us, of course. Fine lot of men the West sends in this time. I'm glad they held the convention in New York; I've never been East before. My name's R. P. Bolder -

Bolder & Son, of Hickory Grove, Missouri."

Though unprepared, I rose to the emergency, as men will when put to it. Now must I hold a christening, and be at once babe, parson and parent. My senses came to the rescue of my slower brain. The insistent odor of drugs from my companion supplied one idea; a glance at his newspaper, where my eye met a *conspicuous* advertisement, assisted me further.

"My name," said I, glibly, "is Edward Pinkhammer. I am a druggist, and my home is in Cornopolis, Kansas."

"I knew you were a druggist," said my fellow traveler, affably. "I saw the callous spot on your right forefinger where the handle of the pestle rubs. Of course, you are a delegate to our National Convention."

"Are all these men druggists?" I asked, wonderingly.

Incommodious
- *Troublesome, inconvenient*
Monogram - *A design of one*
Cinnamon - *A Indian spice*
Pharmaceutists - *Druggists, chemists*

"They are. This car came through from the West. And they're your old-time druggists, too - none of your patent tablet-and-granule *pharmaceutists* that use slot machines instead of a *prescription* desk. We percolate our own paregoric and roll our own pills, and we ain't above handling a few garden seeds in the spring, and carrying a side line of confectionery and shoes.

I tell you Hampinker, I've got an idea to spring on this convention - new ideas is what they want. Now, you know the shelf bottles of *Tartar emetic* and *Rochelle salt* Ant. et Pot. Tart. and Sod. et Pot. Tart. - one's poison, you know, and the other's harmless. It's easy to mistake one label for the other. Where do druggists mostly keep 'em? Why, as far apart as possible, on different shelves. That's wrong. I say keep 'em side by side, so when you want one you can always compare it with the other and avoid mistakes. Do you catch the idea?"

"It seems to me a very good one," I said.

"All right! When I spring it on the convention you back it up. We'll make some of these Eastern orange-phosphate-and-massage-cream professors that think they're the only *lozenges* in the market look like *hypodermic* tablets."

"If I can be of any aid," I said, warming, "the two bottles of - er -"

"Tartrate of antimony and potash, and tartrate of soda and potash."

"Shall henceforth sit side by side," I concluded, firmly.

"Now, there's another thing," said Mr. Bolder. "For an excipient in *manipulating* a pill mass which do you prefer - the magnesia carbonate or the pulverised glycerrhiza radix?"

"The - er - magnesia," I said. It was easier to say than the other word.

Mr. Bolder glanced at me distrustfully through his spectacles.

"Give me the glycerrhiza," said he. "Magnesia cakes."

"Here's another one of these fake aphasia cases," he said, presently, handing me his newspaper, and laying his finger upon an article. "I don't believe in 'em. I put nine out of ten of 'em down as frauds. A man gets sick of his business and his folks and wants to have a good time. He skips out somewhere,

Prescription - *Written instructions form a physician*
Tartar emetic - *Another name for antimony potassium tartrate*
Rochelle salt - *A colourless, white, water soluble soled*
Lozenges - *Toffees*
Hypodermic - *Under the skin*

and when they find him he pretends to have lost his memory - don't know his own name, and won't even recognize the strawberry mark on his wife's left shoulder. Aphasia! Tut! Why can't they stay at home and forget?"

I took the paper and read, after the pungent headlines, the following:

"DENVER, June 12. - Elwyn C. Belford, a prominent lawyer, is mysteriously missing from his home since three days ago, and all efforts to locate him have been in vain. Mr. Bellford is a well-known citizen of the highest standing, and has enjoyed a large and *lucrative* law practice. He is married and owns a fine home and the most extensive private library in the State. On the day of his disappearance, he drew quite a large sum of money from his bank.

No one can be found who saw him after he left the bank. Mr. Bellford was a man of singularly quiet and domestic tastes, and seemed to find his happiness in his home and profession. If any clue at all exists to his strange disappearance, it my be found in the fact that for some months he has been deeply absorbed in an important law case in connection with the Q. Y. and Z. Railroad Company. It is feared that overwork may have affected his mind. Every effort is being made to discover the whereabouts of the missing man."

"It seems to me you are not altogether uncynical, Mr. Bolder," I said, after I had read the despatch. "This has the sound, to me, of a genuine case. Why should this man, prosperous, happily married, and respected, choose suddenly to abandon everything? I know that these lapses of memory do occur, and that men do find themselves *adrift* without a name, a history or a home."

"Oh, gammon and jalap!" said Mr. Bolder. "It's larks they're after. There's too much education nowadays. Men know about aphasia, and they use it for an excuse. The women are wise, too. When it's all over they look you in the eye, as scientific as you please, and say: 'He hypnotised me.'"

Thus Mr. Bolder *diverted*, but did not aid, me with his comments and philosophy.

Lucrative - *Profitable*
Adrift - *Floating without, control*
Diverted - *Deflected, distracted*
Buoyancy - *The power to float*

We arrived in New York about ten at night. I rode in a cab to a hotel, and I wrote my name "Edward Pinkhammer" in the register. As I did so I felt pervade me a splendid, wild, intoxicating *buoyancy* - a sense of unlimited freedom, of newly attained possibilities. I was just born into the world. The old fetters - whatever they had been - were stricken from my hands and feet. The future lay before me a clear road such as an infant enters, and I could set out upon it equipped with a man's learning and experience.

I thought the hotel clerk looked at me five seconds too long. I had no baggage.

"The Druggists' *Convention*," I said. "My trunk has somehow failed to arrive." I drew out a roll of money.

"Ah!" said he, showing an *auriferous* tooth, "we have quite a number of the Western delegates stopping here." He struck a bell for the boy.

I endeavoured to give color to my role.

"There is an important movement on foot among us Westerners," I said, "in regard to a recommendation to the convention that the bottles containing the tartrate of antimony and potash, and the tartrate of sodium and potash be kept in a *contiguous* position on the shelf."

"Gentleman to three-fourteen," said the clerk, hastily. I was whisked away to my room.

The next day I bought a trunk and clothing, and began to live the life of Edward Pinkhammer. I did not tax my brain with endeavours to solve problems of the past.

It was a piquant and sparkling cup that the great island city held up to my lips. I drank of it gratefully. The keys of Manhattan belong to him who is able to bear them. You must be either the city's guest or its victim.

The following few days were as gold and silver. Edward Pinkhammer, yet counting back to his birth by hours only, knew the rare joy of having come upon so diverting a world full-fledged and unrestrained. I sat entranced on the magic carpets provided in theatres and roof-gardens, that transported one into strange and delightful lands full of frolicsome music, pretty girls and *grotesque drolly extravagant parodies* upon human kind.

Auriferous - *Yielding*
Grotesque - *Odd/ unnatural in shape*
Drolly - *Amusing in an odd way*
Parodies - *Mimicries*
Spectacular - *Breath taking*

I went here and there at my own dear will, bound by no limits of space, time or comportment. I dined in weird cabarets, at weirder *tables d'hote* to the sound of Hungarian music and the wild shouts of mercurial artists and sculptors. Or, again, where the night life quivers in the electric glare like a **kinetoscopic** picture, and the millinery of the world, and its jewels, and the ones whom they adorn, and the men who make all three possible are met for good cheer and the **spectacular** effect.

And among all these scenes that I have mentioned I learned one thing that I never knew before. And that is that the key to liberty is not in the hands of License, but Convention holds it. Comity has a toll-gate at which you must pay, or you may not enter the land of Freedom. In all the glitter, the seeming disorder, the parade, the abandon, I saw this law, ***unobtrusive***, yet like iron, prevail. Therefore, in Manhattan you must obey these unwritten laws, and then you will be freest of the free. If you decline to be bound by them, you put on shackles.

Sometimes, as my mood urged me, I would seek the stately, softly murmuring palm rooms, redolent with high-born life and delicate restraint, in which to dine. Again I would go down to the waterways in steamers packed with ***vociferous, bedecked***, unchecked love-making clerks and shop-girls to their crude pleasures on the island shores. And there was always Broadway - glistening, opulent, wily, varying, desirable Broadway - growing upon one like an opium habit.

One afternoon as I entered my hotel a stout man with a big nose and a black moustache blocked my way in the corridor. When I would have passed around him, he greet me with offensive familiarity.

"Hello, Bellford!" he cried, loudly. "What the deuce are you doing in New York? Didn't know anything could drag you away from that old book den of yours. Is Mrs. B. along or is this a little business run alone, eh?"

"You have made a mistake, sir," I said, coldly, releasing my hand from his grasp. "My name is Pinkhammer. You will excuse me."

Unobtrusive - *Not noticeable*
Vociferous - *Crying out noisily*
Bedecked - *Adorned, decorated*
Apparently - *Visible clearly*

The man dropped to one side, ***apparently*** astonished. As I walked to the clerk's desk I heard him call to a bell boy and say something about telegraph blanks.

"You will give me my bill," I said to the clerk, "and have my baggage brought down in half an hour. I do not care to remain where I am annoyed by confidence men."

I moved that afternoon to another hotel, a sedate, old-fashioned one on lower Fifth Avenue.

There was a restaurant a little way off Broadway where one could be served almost *al fresco* in a tropic array of screening flora. Quiet and luxury and a perfect service made it an ideal place in which to take luncheon or refreshment. One afternoon I was there picking my way to a table among the ferns when I felt my sleeve caught.

"Mr. Bellford!" exclaimed an amazingly sweet voice.

I turned quickly to see a lady seated alone - a lady of about thirty, with exceedingly handsome eyes, who looked at me as though I had been her very dear friend.

"You were about to pass me," she said, accusingly. "Don't tell me you do not know me. Why should we not shake hands - at least once in fifteen years?"

I shook hands with her at once. I took a chair opposite her at the table. I summoned with my eyebrows a ***hovering*** waiter. The lady was ***philandering*** with an orange ice. I ordered a *creme de menthe*. Her hair was reddish bronze. You could not look at it, because you could not look away from her eyes. But you were conscious of it as you are conscious of sunset while you look into the ***profundities*** of a wood at twilight.

"Are you sure you know me?" I asked.

"No," she said, smiling. "I was never sure of that."

"What would you think," I said, a little anxiously, "if I were to tell you that my name is Edward Pinkhammer, from Cornopolis, Kansas?"

"What would I think?" she repeated, with a merry glance. "Why, that you had not brought Mrs. Bellford to New York with you, of course. I do wish you had. I would have liked to see Marian." Her voice lowered slightly - "You haven't changed much, Elwyn."

Hovering - *Lingering about*
Philandering - *Flirting*
Flouted - *To show contempts*
Timorously - *Fearful*

I felt her wonderful eyes searching mine and my face more closely.

"Yes, you have," she amended, and there was a soft, exultant note in her latest tones; "I see it now. You haven't forgotten. You haven't forgotten for a year or a day or an hour. I told you you never could."

I poked my straw anxiously in the *creme de menthe*.

"I'm sure I beg your pardon," I said, a little uneasy at her gaze. "But that is just the trouble. I have forgotten. I've forgotten everything."

She *flouted* my denial. She laughed deliciously at something she seemed to see in my face.

"I've heard of you at times," she went on. "You're quite a big lawyer out West - Denver, isn't it, or Los Angeles? Marian must be very proud of you. You knew, I suppose, that I married six months after you did. You may have seen it in the papers. The flowers alone cost two thousand dollars."

She had mentioned fifteen years. Fifteen years is a long time.

"Would it be too late," I asked, somewhat timorously, "to offer you congratulations?"

"Not if you dare do it," she answered, with such fine ***intrepidity*** that I was silent, and began to crease patterns on the cloth with my thumb nail.

"Tell me one thing," she said, leaning toward me rather eagerly - "a thing I have wanted to know for many years - just from a woman's curiosity, of course - have you ever dared since that night to touch, smell or look at white roses - at white roses wet with rain and dew?"

I took a sip of *creme de menthe*.

"It would be useless, I suppose," I said, with a sigh, "for me to repeat that I have no recollection at all about these things. My memory is completely at fault. I need not say how much I regret it."

The lady rested her arms upon the table, and again her eyes ***disdained*** my words and went traveling by their own route direct to my soul. She laughed softly, with a strange quality in the sound - it was a laugh of happiness - yes, and of content - and of misery. I tried to look away from her.

Intrepidity -
Disdained -
Concede -
Delegates -

"You lie, Elwyn Bellford," she breathed, blissfully. "Oh, I know you lie!"

I gazed dully into the ferns.

"My name is Edward Pinkhammer," I said. "I came with the *delegates* to the Druggists' National Convention. There is a movement on foot for arranging a new position for the bottles of tartrate of antimony and tartrate of potash, in which, very likely, you would take little interest."

A shining landau stopped before the entrance. The lady rose. I took her hand, and bowed.

"I am deeply sorry," I said to her, "that I cannot remember. I could explain, but fear you would not understand. You will not concede Pinkhammer; and I really cannot at all conceive of the - the roses and other things."

"Good-by, Mr. Bellford," she said, with her happy, sorrowful smile, as she stepped into her carriage.

I attended the theatre that night. When I returned to my hotel, a quiet man in dark clothes, who seemed interested in rubbing his finger nails with a silk handkerchief, appeared, magically, at my side.

"Mr. Pinkhammer," he said, giving the bulk of his attention to his forefinger, "may I request you to step aside with me for a little conversation? There is a room here."

"Certainly," I answered.

He conducted me into a small, private parlour. A lady and a gentleman were there. The lady, I surmised, would have been unusually good-looking had her features not been clouded by an expression of keen worry and fatigue. She was of a style of figure and possessed colouring and features that were agreeable to my fancy. She was in a travelling dress; she fixed upon me an earnest look of extreme *anxiety*, and pressed an unsteady hand to her bosom. I think she would have started forward, but the gentleman arrested her movement with an authoritative motion of his hand. He then came, himself, to meet me. He was a man of forty, a little grey about the temples, and with a strong, thoughtful face.

"Bellford, old man," he said, cordially, "I'm glad to see you again. Of course we know everything is all right. I warned you,

Wearisome - *Tiresome*
Wailing - *Crying loudly*
Detaining - *To keep under restraint*
Allusion - *A passing*
Moaned - *Sound of pain*

you know, that you were overdoing it. Now, you'll go back with us, and be yourself again in no time."

I smiled ironically.

"I have been 'Bellforded' so often," I said, "that it has lost its edge. Still, in the end, it may grow wearisome. Would you be willing at all to entertain the hypothesis that my name is Edward Pinkhammer, and that I never saw you before in my life?"

Before the man could reply a wailing cry came from the woman. She sprang past his detaining arm. "Elwyn!" she sobbed, and cast herself upon me, and clung tight. "Elwyn," she cried again, "don't break my heart. I am your wife - call my name once - just once. I could see you dead rather than this way."

I unwound her arms respectfully, but firmly.

"Madam," I said, severely, "pardon me if I suggest that you accept a resemblance too precipitately. It is a pity," I went on, with an amused laugh, as the thought occurred to me, "that this Bellford and I could not be kept side by side upon the same shelf like tartrates of sodium and antimony for purposes of identification. In order to understand the allusion," I concluded airily, "it may be necessary for you to keep an eye on the proceedings of the Druggists' National Convention."

The lady turned to her companion, and grasped his arm.

"What is it, Doctor Volney? Oh, what is it?" she moaned.

"Go to your room for a while," I heard him say. "I will remain and talk with him. His mind? No, I think not - only a portion of the brain. Yes, I am sure he will recover. Go to your room and leave me with him."

The lady disappeared. The man in dark clothes also went outside, still *manicuring* himself in a thoughtful way. I think he waited in the hall.

"I would like to talk with you a while, Mr. Pinkhammer, if I may," said the gentleman who remained.

"Very well, if you care to," I replied, "and will excuse me if I take it comfortably; I am rather tired." I stretched myself upon a *couch* by a window and lit a cigar. He drew a chair nearby.

"Let us speak to the point," he said, *soothingly*. "Your name is not Pinkhammer."

Manicuring - *A cosmetic treatment of the hands*
Couch - *A bed*
Soothingly - *Calmingly*
Extravagantly - *Spending more than necessary*
Christens - *To give name to at baptism*

"I know that as well as you do," I said, coolly. "But a man must have a name of some sort. I can assure you that I do not *extravagantly* admire the name of Pinkhammer. But when one christens one's self suddenly, the fine names do not seem to suggest themselves. But, suppose it had been Scheringhausen or Scroggins! I think I did very well with Pinkhammer."

"Your name," said the other man, seriously, "is Elwyn C. Bellford. You are one of the first lawyers in Denver. You are suffering from an attack of aphasia, which has caused you to forget your identity. The cause of it was over-application to your profession, and, perhaps, a life too bare of natural recreation and pleasures. The lady who has just left the room is your wife."

"She is what I would call a fine-looking woman," I said, after a judicial pause. "I particularly admire the shade of brown in her hair."

"She is a wife to be proud of. Since your disappearance, nearly two weeks ago, she has scarcely closed her eyes. We learned that you were in New York through a telegram sent by Isidore Newman, a traveling man from Denver. He said that he had met you in a hotel here, and that you did not recognise him."

"I think I remember the occasion," I said. "The fellow called me 'Bellford,' if I am not mistaken. But don't you think it about time, now, for you to introduce yourself?"

"I am Robert Volney - Doctor Volney. I have been your close friend for twenty years, and your physician for fifteen. I came with Mrs. Bellford to trace you as soon as we got the telegram. Try, Elwyn, old man - try to remember!"

"What's the use to try?" I asked, with a little frown. "You say you are a physician. Is aphasia curable? When a man loses his memory does it return slowly, or suddenly?"

"Sometimes gradually and imperfectly; sometimes as suddenly as it went."

"Will you undertake the treatment of my case, Doctor Volney?" I asked.

"Old friend," said he, "I'll do everything in my power, and will have done everything that science can do to cure you."

"Very well," said I. "Then you will consider that I am your patient. Everything is in confidence now - professional confidence."

Frown - *To contract the brow*
Sprinkled - *Scattered in drops*
Fragrant - *Having a pleasant*
Shin - *The front part of the leg*

"Of course," said Doctor Volney.

I got up from the couch. Some one had set a vase of white roses on the centre table - a cluster of white roses, freshly sprinkled and fragrant. I threw them far out of the window, and then laid myself upon the couch again.

"It will be best, Bobby," I said, "to have this cure happen suddenly. I'm rather tired of it all, anyway. You may go now and bring Marian in. But, oh, Doc," I said, with a sigh, as I kicked him on the shin - "good old Doc - it was glorious!"

Food For Thought

" I got up from the couch. Somone had set a vase of white roses on the centre table - I threw them far out of the window , and then laid myself upon the couch again." Do you think the bun ch of white roses brought back Belford's memory, or Belford never had any attack of Aphasis, he just was tired and sick of his routine life wanting some change. Support your answer with relevant reasons.

An Understanding

Q. 1. What is Aphasia in a common man's language? How does it affect a person and what happens after the attack? Which organ of the body is affected by this attack?
Ans. _____
_____
_____
_____
_____

Q. 2. How did Aphasia attack Belford's memory and how did it change his life and profession? Who was belford and how was his life before the attack?
Ans. _____
_____
_____
_____
_____

Q. 3. What were the warnings given by Belford's friend and family doctor, Volney? What measures did Dr. Volney suggest to prevent the attack of Aphasia?
Ans. _____
_____
_____
_____
_____

Q. 5. What name did Belford think of and which profession did he choose after the attack of Aphasia? Where did he land into and where was he? Whom all did he meet during his illness and how did he behave?
Ans. _____
_____
_____
_____
_____

My Favourite Murder
~ Ambrose Bierce

Having murdered my mother under circumstances of singular atrocity, I was arrested and put upon my trial, which lasted seven years. In charging the jury, the judge of the Court of *Acquittal* remarked that it was one of the most ghastly crimes that he had ever been called upon to explain away.

At this, my attorney rose and said:

"May it please your Honour, crimes are ghastly or agreeable only by comparison. If you were familiar with the details of my client's previous murder of his uncle you would discern in his later offence (if offence it may be called) something in the nature of tender forbearance and *filial* consideration for the feelings of the victim. The *appalling ferocity* of the former assassination was indeed *inconsistent* with any hypothesis but that of guilt; and had it not been for the fact that the honourable judge before whom he was tried was the president of a life insurance company that took risks on hanging, and in which my client held a policy, it is hard to see how he could decently have been acquitted. If your Honour would like to hear about it for instruction and guidance of your Honour's mind, this unfortunate man, my client, will consent to give himself the pain of relating it under oath."

The district *attorney* said: "Your Honour, I object. Such a statement would be in the nature of evidence, and the testimony in this case is closed. The prisoner's statement should have been introduced three years ago, in the spring of 1881."

"In a statutory sense," said the judge, "you are right, and in the Court of Objections and Technicalities you would get a ruling in your favor. But not in a Court of *Acquittal*. The objection is overruled."

"I except," said the district attorney.

"You cannot do that," the judge said. "I must remind you that in order to take an *exception* you must first get this case transferred for a time to the Court of Exceptions on a formal motion duly supported by *affidavits*. A motion to that effect by your *predecessor* in office was denied by me during the first year of this trial. Mr. Clerk, swear the prisoner."

Filial - *Pertaining to*
Appaling - *To fill*
Acquittal - *Discharge*
Exceptions - *Something excepted*
Predecessor - *Succeeds*

The customary oath having been administered, I made the following following statement, which *impressed* the judge with so strong a sense of the comparative triviality of the offence for which I was on trial that he made no further search for mitigating circumstances, but simply instructed the jury to acquit, and I left the court, without a stain upon my reputation:

"I was born in 1856 in Kalamakee, Mich., of honest and *reputable* parents, one of whom Heaven has mercifully spared to comfort me in my later years. In 1867 the family came to California and settled near Nigger Head, where my father opened a road agency and prospered beyond the dreams of avarice. He was a reticent, saturnine man then, though his increasing years have now somewhat relaxed the austerity of his disposition, and I believe that nothing but his memory of the sad event for which I am now on trial prevents him from manifesting a genuine *hilarity*.

"Four years after we had set up the road agency an *itinerant* preacher came along, and having no other way to pay for the night's lodging that we gave him, favored us with an exhortation of such power that, praise God, we were all converted to religion. My father at once sent for his brother the Hon. William Ridley of Stockton, and on his arrival turned over the agency to him, charging him nothing for the franchise nor plant - the latter consisting of a Winchester rifle, a sawed-off shotgun, and an *assortment* of masks made out of flour sacks. The family then moved to Ghost Rock and opened a dance house. It was called 'The Saints' Rest Hurdy-Gurdy,' and the proceedings each night began with prayer. It was there that my now sainted mother, by her grace in the dance, acquired the *sobriquet* of 'The Bucking Walrus.'

"In the fall of '75 I had occasion to visit Coyote, on the road to Mahala, and took the stage at Ghost Rock. There were four other passengers. About three miles beyond Nigger Head, persons whom I identified as my Uncle William and his two sons held up the stage. Finding nothing in the express box, they went through the passengers. I acted a most honourable part in the affair, placing myself in line with the others, holding up my hands and permitting myself to be *deprived* of forty dollars and a gold watch. From my behavior no one could have suspected that I knew the gentlemen who gave the entertainment. A few days later, when I went to Nigger Head and asked for the return of my money and watch my uncle

Impressed -
Fascinated
Reputable -
Honorarily
Hilarity -
Cheerfulness
Itinerant - *Travelling form place to place*
Assortment - *A collection*
Sobriquet -
Nickname

and cousins swore they knew nothing of the matter, and they affected a belief that my father and I had done the job ourselves in dishonest violation of commercial good faith. Uncle William even threatened to *retaliate* by starting an opposition dance house at Ghost Rock. As 'The Saints' Rest' had become rather unpopular, I saw that this would assuredly ruin it and prove a paying enterprise, so I told my uncle that I was willing to overlook the past if he would take me into the scheme and keep the partnership a secret from my father. This fair offer he rejected, and I then perceived that it would be better and more satisfactory if he were dead.

"My plans to that end were soon perfected, and communicating them to my dear parents I had the ***gratification*** of receiving their approval. My father said he was proud of me, and my mother promised that although her religion forbade her to assist in taking human life I should have the advantage of her prayers for my success. As a preliminary measure looking to my security in case of ***detection*** I made an application for membership in that powerful order, the Knights of Murder, and in due course was received as a member of the Ghost Rock ***commandery***. On the day that my probation ended I was for the first time permitted to inspect the records of the order and learn who belonged to it - all the rites of initiation having been conducted in masks. Fancy my delight when, in looking over the roll of membership, I found the third name to be that of my uncle, who indeed was junior vice-chancellor of the order! Here was an opportunity exceeding my wildest dreams - to murder I could add insubordination and treachery. It was what my good mother would have called 'a special Providence.'

"At about this time something occurred which caused my cup of joy, already full, to overflow on all sides, a circular cataract of bliss. Three men, strangers in that locality, were arrested for the stage robbery in which I had lost my money and watch. They were brought to trial and, despite my efforts to clear them and fasten the guilt upon three of the most respectable and worthy citizens of Ghost Rock, convicted on the clearest proof. The murder would now be as wanton and reasonless as I could wish.

"One morning I shouldered my Winchester rifle, and going over to my uncle's house, near Nigger Head, asked my Aunt Mary, his wife, if he were at home, adding that I had

Retaliate - *To reciprocate, repay*
Gratification - *Great satisfaction*
Detection - *The act of discovering*
Commandery - *The office*

come to kill him. My aunt replied with her peculiar smile that so many gentleman called on that *errand* and were afterward carried away without having performed it that I must excuse her for doubting my good faith in the matter. She said I did not look as if I would kill anybody, so, as a proof of good faith I levelled my rifle and wounded a Chinaman who happened to be passing the house. She said she knew whole families that could do a thing of that kind, but Bill Ridley was a horse of another colour. She said, however, that I would find him over on the other side of the *creek* in the sheep lot; and she added that she hoped the best man would win.

"My Aunt Mary was one of the most fair-minded women that I have ever met.

"I found my uncle down on his knees engaged in skinning a sheep. Seeing that he had neither gun nor pistol handy I had not the heart to shoot him, so I approached him, greeted him pleasantly and struck him a powerful blow on the head with the butt of my rifle. I have a very good delivery and Uncle William lay down on his side, then rolled over on his back, spread out his fingers and shivered. Before he could recover the use of his limbs I seized the knife that he had been using and cut his hamstrings. You know, doubtless, that when you sever the Achilles tendon, the patient has no further use of his leg; it is just the same as if he had no leg. Well, I parted them both, and when he *revived* he was at my service. As soon as he *comprehended* the situation, he said:

" 'Samuel, you have got the drop on me and can afford to be generous. I have only one thing to ask of you, and that is that you carry me to the house and finish me in the bosom of my family.'

"I told him I thought that a pretty reasonable request and I would do so if he would let me put him into a wheat sack; he would be easier to carry that way and if we were seen by the neighbours en route it would cause less remark. He agreed to that, and going to the barn I got a sack. This, however, did not fit him; it was too short and much wider than he; so I bent his legs, forced his knees up against his breast and got him into it that way, tying the sack above his head. He was a heavy man and I had all that I could do to get him on my back, but I *staggered* along for some distance until I came to a swing that some of the children had suspended to the branch of an oak. Here I laid him down and sat upon him to rest, and the sight

Errand - *A short and quick trip*
Creek - *A stream*
Comprehended - *Perceived*
Staggered - *To walk/move*
Revived - *To restore to life, vigour*

of the rope gave me a happy inspiration. In twenty minutes my uncle, still in the sack, swung free to the sport of the wind.

"I had taken down the rope, tied one end tightly about the mouth of the bag, thrown the other across the limb and **hauled** him up about five feet from the ground. Fastening the other end of the rope also about the mouth of the sack, I had the satisfaction to see my uncle converted into a large, fine pendulum. I must add that he was not himself entirely aware of the nature of the change that he had undergone in his relation to the exterior world, though in justice to a good man's memory I ought to say that I do not think he would in any case have wasted much of my time in vain *remonstrance*.

"Uncle William had a ram that was famous in all that region as a fighter. It was in a state of chronic constitutional indignation. Some deep disappointment in early life had soured its disposition and it had declared war upon the whole world. To say that it would butt anything accessible is but faintly to express the nature and scope of its military activity: the universe was its antagonist; its methods that of a projectile. It fought like the angels and devils, in mid-air, cleaving the atmosphere like a bird, describing a *parabolic* curve and descending upon its victim at just the exact angle of incidence to make the most of its velocity and weight. Its momentum, calculated in foot-tons, was something incredible. It had been seen to destroy a four year old bull by a single impact upon that animal's gnarly forehead. No stone wall had ever been known to resist its downward swoop; there were no trees tough enough to stay it; it would splinter them into matchwood and defile their leafy honours in the dust. This *irascible* and *implacable* brute - this *incarnate* thunderbolt - this monster of the upper deep, I had seen reposing in the shade of an adjacent tree, dreaming dreams of conquest and glory. It was with a view to summoning it forth to the field of honour that I suspended its master in the manner described.

"Having completed my preparations, I imparted to the *avuncular* pendulum a gentle oscillation, and retiring to cover behind a contiguous rock, lifted up my voice in a long rasping cry whose diminishing final note was drowned in a noise like that of a swearing cat, which *emanated* from the sack. Instantly that *formidable* sheep was upon its feet and had taken in the military situation at a glance. In a few moments it had approached, stamping, to within fifty yards of the swinging foeman, who, now retreating and anon advancing, seemed to invite

Hauled - *To pull/ draw with force*
Remonstrance - *A protest*
Parabolic - *Pertaining to*
Incarnate - *Personified*
Implacable - *Unappeasable*
Avuncular - *Resembling an uncle*
Formidable - *Powerfull, of great strength*

the fray. Suddenly I saw the beast's head drop earthward as if depressed by the weight of its enormous horns; then a dim, white, wavy streak of sheep prolonged itself from that spot in a generally horizontal direction to within about four yards of a point immediately beneath the enemy. There it struck sharply upward, and before it had faded from my gaze at the place whence it had set out I heard a horrid thump and a piercing scream, and my poor uncle shot forward, with a slack rope higher than the limb to which he was attached. Here the rope tautened with a jerk, arresting his flight, and back he swung in a breathless curve to the other end of his arc. The ram had fallen, a heap of indistinguishable legs, wool and horns, but pulling itself together and dodging as its antagonist swept downward it retired at random, alternately shaking its head and stamping its fore-feet. When it had backed about the same distance as that from which it had delivered the assault it paused again, bowed its head as if in prayer for victory and again shot forward, dimly visible as before - a prolonging white streak with monstrous undulations, ending with a sharp ascension. Its course this time was at a right angle to its former one, and its impatience so great that it struck the enemy before he had nearly reached the lowest point of his arc. In consequence he went flying round and round in a horizontal circle whose radius was about equal to half the length of the rope, which I forgot to say was nearly twenty feet long. His shrieks, crescendo in approach and diminuendo in recession, made the rapidity of his revolution more obvious to the ear than to the eye. He had evidently not yet been struck in a vital spot. His posture in the sack and the distance from the ground at which he hung compelled the ram to operate upon his lower extremities and the end of his back. Like a plant that has struck its root into some poisonous mineral, my poor uncle was dying slowly upward.

"After delivering its second blow the ram had not again retired. The fever of battle burned hot in its heart; its brain was intoxicated with the wine of strife. Like a pugilist who in his rage forgets his skill and fights ineffectively at half-arm's length, the angry beast endeavored to reach its fleeting foe by awkward vertical leaps as he passed overhead, sometimes, indeed, succeeding in striking him feebly, but more frequently overthrown by its own misguided eagerness. But as the impetus was exhausted and the man's circles narrowed in scope and diminished in speed, bringing him nearer to the ground, these tactics produced better

Antagonist - *Opponent*
Diminuendo - *Gradually reducing in force*
Compelled - *Forced*
Pugilist - *Boxer*
Endeavoured - *Ventured*
Tactics - *Plan*

results, eliciting a superior quality of screams, which I greatly enjoyed.

"Suddenly, as if the bugles had sung truce, the ram suspended hostilities and walked away, thoughtfully wrinkling and smoothing its great aquiline nose, and occasionally cropping a bunch of grass and slowly munching it. It seemed to have tired of war's alarms and resolved to beat the sword into a plowshare and cultivate the arts of peace. Steadily it held its course away from the field of fame until it had gained a distance of nearly a quarter of a mile. There it stopped and stood with its rear to the foe, chewing its cud and apparently half asleep. I observed, however, an occasional slight turn of its head, as if its apathy were more affected than real.

"Meantime Uncle William's shrieks had abated with his motion, and nothing was heard from him but long, low moans, and at long intervals my name, uttered in pleading tones exceedingly grateful to my ear. Evidently the man had not the faintest notion of what was being done to him, and was inexpressibly terrified. When Death comes cloaked in mystery he is terrible indeed. Little by little my uncle's oscillations diminished, and finally, he hung motionless. I went to him and was about to give him the coup de grace, when I heard and felt a succession of smart shocks which shook the ground like a series of light earthquakes, and turning in the direction of the ram, saw a long cloud of dust approaching me with inconceivable rapidity and alarming effect! At a distance of some thirty yards away it stopped short, and from the near end of it rose into the air what I at first thought a great white bird. Its ascent was so smooth and easy and regular that I could not realize its extraordinary celerity, and was lost in admiration of its grace. To this day the impression remains that it was a slow, deliberate movement, the ram - for it was that animal - being upborne by some power other than its own impetus, and supported through the successive stages of its flight with infinite tenderness and care. My eyes followed its progress through the air with unspeakable pleasure, all the greater by contrast with my former terror of its approach by land. Onward and upward the noble animal sailed, its head bent down almost between its knees, its fore-feet thrown back, its hinder legs trailing to rear like the legs of a soaring heron.

"At a height of forty or fifty feet, as fond recollection presents it to view, it attained its *zenith* and appeared to remain an instant stationary; then, tilting suddenly forward without

Bugies - *Bugle*
Truce - *Peace*
Aquiline - *Shaped like an eagle*
Cud - *Beak*
Inconceivable - *Unbelievable*
Celerity - *Swiftness*

altering the relative position of its parts, it shot downward on a steeper and steeper course with augmenting velocity, passed immediately above me with a noise like the rush of a cannon shot and struck my poor uncle almost squarely on the top of the head! So frightful was the impact that not only the man's neck was broken, but the rope too; and the body of the ***deceased***, forced against the earth, was crushed to pulp beneath the awful front of that meteoric sheep! The concussion stopped all the clocks between Lone Hand and Dutch Dan's, and Professor Davidson, a distinguished authority in matters ***seismic***, who happened to be in the vicinity, promptly explained that the vibrations were from north to southwest.

"Altogether, I cannot help thinking that in point of artistic ***atrocity*** my murder of Uncle William has seldom been excelled."

Deceased - *No longer living, dead*
Atrocity - *Cruelty*
Seismic - *Relating to*

Food For Thought

How do you like this story? Do you feel that the story is humorous or a serious one? How do you like the ending of the story? Can you suggest some other possible ending to the story?

An Understanding

Q. 1. Why was the narrator arrested and put upon trial for seven years?
Ans. _____
_____
_____
_____
_____

Q. 2. Why did the narrator's attorney rise up when the judge of the court of Acquittal remarked that it was one of the most ghastly crimes that he had ever been called upon to explain?
Ans. _____
_____
_____
_____
_____

Q. 3. How and why did the narrator kill his uncle? Why do you think that the story is humorous when the narrator's attorney describes the narrator's previous murder as more ghastly than his present one? Explain.
Ans. _____
_____
_____
_____
_____

Q. 4. Why does the narrator describe his uncle's murder as his favourite murder? What were the atrocities which the narrator's uncle committed towards the narrator and his parents that compelled the narrator to kill him?
Ans. _____
_____
_____
_____
_____

A Bread And Butter Miss
~Saki

"Starling Chatter and Oakhill have both dropped back in the betting," said Bertie van Tahn, throwing the morning paper across the breakfast table.

"That leaves Nursery Tea practically favourite," said Odo Finsberry.

"Nursery Tea and Pipeclay are at the top of the betting at present," said Bertie, "but that French horse, Le Five O'Clock, seems to be *fancied* as much as anything. Then there is Whitebait, and the Polish horse with a name like some one trying to *stifle* a sneeze in church; they both seem to have a lot of support."

"It's the most open Derby there's been for years," said Odo.

"It's simply no good trying to pick the winner on form," said Bertie; "one must just trust to luck and inspiration."

"The question is whether to trust to one's own inspiration, or somebody else's. Sporting Swank gives Count Palatine to win, and Le Five O'Clock for a place."

"Count Palatine -- that adds another to our list of perplexities. Good morning, Sir Lulworth; have you a fancy for the Derby by any chance?"

"I don't usually take much interest in turf matters," said Sir Lulworth, who had just made his appearance, "but I always like to have a bet on the Guineas and the Derby. This year, I confess, it's rather difficult to pick out anything that seems markedly better than anything else. What do you think of Snow Bunting?"

"Snow Bunting?" said Odo, with a groan, "there's another of them. Surely, Snow Bunting has no earthly chance?"

"My housekeeper's nephew, who is a shoeing-smith in the mounted section of the Church Lads' Brigade, and an authority on horseflesh, expects him to be among the first three."

"The nephews of housekeepers are invariably optimists," said Bertie; "it's a kind of natural reaction against the professional *pessimism* of their aunts."

"We don't seem to get much further in our search for the *probable* winner," said Mrs. de Claux; "the more I listen to you experts the more hopelessly *befogged* I get."

"It's all very well to blame us," said Bertie to his hostess; "you haven't produced anything in the way of an inspiration."

Fancied - *Imagined*
Stifle - *To quell*
Pessimism - *The tendency to expect the worst*
Probable - *Likely to occur*
Befogged - *Confounded*

"My inspiration consisted in asking you down for Derby week," *retorted* Mrs. de Claux; "I thought you and Odo between you might throw some light on the question of the moment."

Further *recriminations* were cut short by the arrival of Lola Pevensey, who floated into the room with an air of gracious apology.

"So sorry to be so late," she observed, making a rapid tour of *inspection* of the breakfast dishes. "Did you have a good night?" asked her hostess with perfunctory solicitude.

"Quite, thank you," said Lola; "I dreamt a most remarkable dream."

A flutter, indicative of general *boredom*; went round the table. Other people's dreams are about as universally interesting as accounts of other people's gardens, or chickens, or children. "I dreamt about the winner of the Derby," said Lola.

A swift reaction of attentive interest set in.

"Do tell us what you dreamt," came in a chorus.

"The really remarkable thing about it is that I've dreamt it two nights running," said Lola, finally deciding between the **allurements** of sausages and **kedgeree**; "that is why I thought it worth mentioning. You know, when I dream things two or three nights in succession, it always means something; I have special powers in that way. For instance, I once dreamed three times that a winged lion was flying through the sky and one of his wings dropped off, and he came to the ground with a crash; just afterwards the Campanile at Venice fell down. The winged lion is the symbol of Venice, you know," she added for the enlightenment of those who might not be versed in Italian heraldry. "Then," she continued, "just before the murder of the King and Queen of Servia I had a vivid dream of two crowned figures walking into a slaughter-house by the banks of a big river, which I took to be the Danube; and only the other day --"

"Do tell us what you've dreamt about the Derby," interrupted Odo impatiently.

"Well, I saw the finish of the race as clearly as anything; and one horse won easily, almost in a *canter*, and everybody cried out 'Bread and Butter wins! Good old Bread and Butter.' I heard the name distinctly, and I've had the same dream two nights running."

"Bread and Butter," said Mrs. de Claux, "now, whatever horse can that point to? Why -- of course; Nursery Tea!"

Retorted - *To reply to*
Recriminations - *To return accusations*
Boredom - *Dullness, wearness*
Allurements - *Charms*
Kedgeree - *A cooked dish of rice, fish, hard-boiled eggs*
Canter - *An easy gallop*

She looked round with the triumphant smile of a successful *unraveller* of mystery.

"How about Le Five O'Clock?" *interposed* Sir Lulworth.

"It would fit either of them equally well," said Odo; "can you remember any details about the jockey's colours? That might help us."

"I seem to remember a glimpse of lemon sleeves or cap, but I can't be sure," said Lola, after due reflection.

"There isn't a lemon jacket or cap in the race," said Bertie, referring to a list of starters and jockeys; "can't you remember anything about the appearance of the horse? If it were a thick-set animal, this bread and butter would typify Nursery Tea; and if it were thin, of course, it would mean Le Five O'Clock."

"That seems sound enough," said Mrs. de Claux; "do think, Lola dear, whether the horse in your dream was thin or stoutly built."

"I can't remember that it was one or the other," said Lola; "one wouldn't notice such a detail in the excitement of a finish."

"But this was a symbolic animal," said Sir Lulworth; "if it were to *typify* thick or thin bread and butter surely it ought to have been either as bulky and *tubby* as a shire cart-horse; or as thin as a heraldic leopard."

"I'm afraid you are rather a careless dreamer," said Bertie *resentfully*.

"Of course, at the moment of dreaming I thought I was witnessing a real race, not the portent of one," said Lola; "otherwise I should have particularly noticed all helpful details."

"The Derby isn't run till to-morrow," said Mrs. de Claux; "do you think you are likely to have the same dream again to-night? If so; you can fix your attention on the important detail of the animal's appearance."

"I'm afraid I shan't sleep at all to-night," said Lola pathetically; "every fifth night I suffer from *insomnia*, and it's due to-night."

"It's most *provoking*," said Bertie; "of course, we can back both horses, but it would be much more satisfactory to have all our money on the winner. Can't you take a sleeping-draught, or something?"

"Oakleaves, soaked in warm water and put under the bed, are recommended by some," said Mrs. de Claux.

Unraveller - *To free from complication*
Interposed - *To place between*
Typify - *Short and fat*

"A glass of **Benedictine**, with a drop of eau-de-Cologne --" said Sir Lulworth.

"I have tried every known remedy," said Lola, with dignity; "I've been a *martyr* to insomnia for years."

"But now we are being martyrs to it," said Odo sulkily; "I particularly want to land a big coup over this race."

"I don't have insomnia for my own amusement," snapped Lola.

"Let us hope for the best," said Mrs. de Claux soothingly; "to-night may prove an exception to the fifth-night rule."

But when breakfast time came round again Lola reported a blank night as far as visions were concerned.

"I don't suppose I had as much as ten minutes' sleep, and, certainly, no dreams."

"I'm so sorry, for your sake in the first place, and ours as well," said her hostess; "do you think you could induce a short *nap* after breakfast? It would be so good for you -- and you *might* dream something. There would still be time for us to get our bets on."

"I'll try if you like," said Lola; "it sounds rather like a small child being sent to bed in *disgrace*." "I'll come and read the Encyclopaedia Britannica to you if you think it will make you sleep any sooner," said Bertie obligingly.

Rain was falling too steadily to permit of outdoor amusement, and the party suffered considerably during the next two hours from the absolute quiet that was enforced all over the house in order to give Lola every chance of achieving slumber. Even the click of billiard balls was considered a possible factor of disturbance, and the canaries were carried down to the gardener's lodge, while the cuckoo clock in the hall was muffled under several layers of rugs. A notice, "Please do not Knock or Ring," was posted on the front door at Bertie's suggestion, and guests and servants spoke in tragic whispers as though the dread presence of death or sickness had invaded the house. The precautions proved of no *avail*: Lola added a sleepless morning to a *wakeful* night, and the bets of the party had to be *impartially* divided between Nursery Tea and the French *Colt*.

"So provoking to have to split out bets," said Mrs. de Claux, as her guests gathered in the hall later in the day, waiting for the result of the race.

Provoking - *Enraging, vexing*
Benedictine - *A monk*
Martyr - *A person who suffers death*
Nap - *Doze, to sleep for a short time*
Disgrace - *The less of respect*

Greatest Humour Stories

"I did my best for you," said Lola, feeling that she was not getting her due share of gratitude; "I told you what I had seen in my dreams, a brown horse, called Bread and Butter, winning easily from all the rest."

"What?" screamed Bertie, jumping up from his sea, "a brown horse! Miserable woman, you never said a word about it's being a brown horse."

"Didn't I?" faltered Lola; "I thought I told you it was a brown horse. It was certainly brown in both dreams. But I don't see what the colour has got to do with it. Nursery Tea and Le Five O'Clock are both *chestnuts*."

"Merciful Heaven! Doesn't brown bread and butter with a sprinkling of lemon in the colours suggest anything to you?" raged Bertie.

A slow, *cumulative* groan broke from the assembly as the meaning of his words gradually dawned on his hearers.

For the second time that day Lola retired to the seclusion of her room; she could not face the universal looks of reproach directed at her when Whitebait was announced winner at the comfortable price of fourteen to one.

Wakeful - *Watchful, alert*
Colt - *A young male animal of the horse family*
Chestnuts - *Edible nuts tree*
Cumulative - *Growing in quanfity*
Dawned - *To begin to open*
Seclusion - *Solitude*

Food For Thought

Who won the Derby horse-race finally? What was the reaction of Lola and others? Do you believe in betting? Do you feel it's a good pastime or hobby? Support you answer with appropriate reasons.

An Understanding

Q. 1. What were Starling Chatter, Oakhill Nursry Tea and Pipeclay including Whitebait, who won the Derby? Who was the hostess of the party?
Ans. _____
_____
_____
_____
_____

Q. 2. Which two horses were at the top of the betting according to Bertie?
Ans. _____
_____
_____
_____
_____

Q. 3. Why did Odo and Bertie support the idea that the present Derby horse-racing was an open one and there was no point betting?
Ans. _____
_____
_____
_____
_____

Q. 4. Why was the hostess disappointed by the discussion that went round the table? Who was Lola and what did she dream about the winner of the Derby?
Ans. _____
_____
_____
_____
_____

A Night In New Arabia
~ O. Henry

The great city of Bagdad-on-the-Subway is caliph-ridden. Its palaces, bazaars, khans, and byways are thronged with Al Rashids in divers disguises, seeking diversion and victims for their unbridled generosity. You can scarcely find a poor beggar whom they are willing to let enjoy his spoils *unsuccored*, nor a *wrecked* unfortunate upon whom they will not reshower the means of fresh misfortune. You will hardly find anywhere a hungry one who has not had the opportunity to tighten his belt in gift libraries, nor a poor pundit who has not blushed at the holiday basket of celery-crowned turkey forced *resoundingly* through his door by the *eleemosynary* press.

So then, fearfully through the Harun-haunted streets creep the one-eyed calenders, the Little Hunchback and the Barber's Sixth Brother, hoping to escape the ministrations of the roving *horde* of *caliphoid* sultans.

Entertainment for many Arabian nights might be had from the histories of those who have escaped the largesse of the army of Commanders of the Faithful. Until dawn you might sit on the enchanted rug and listen to such stories as are told of the powerful genie Roc-Ef-El-Er who sent the Forty Thieves to soak up the oil plant of Ali Baba; of the good Caliph Kar-Neg-Ghe, who gave away palaces; of the Seven Voyages of Sailbad, the Sinner, who frequented wooden excursion steamers among the islands; of the Fisherman and the Bottle; of the Barmecides' Boarding house; of Aladdin's rise to wealth by means of his Wonderful Gasmeter.

But now, there being ten sultans to one Sheherazade, she is held too valuable to be in fear of the bowstring. In consequence the art of narrative languishes. And, as the lesser caliphs are hunting the happy poor and the resigned unfortunate from cover to cover in order to heap upon them strange mercies and mysterious benefits, too often comes the report from Arabian headquarters that the captive refused "to talk."

This reticence, then, in the actors who perform the sad comedies of their philanthropy-scourged world, must, in a

Unsuccored - *Without help*
Wrecked - *Reduce a slate run*
Resoundingly - *Uttered loudly*
Eleemosynary - *Derived from*
Harun - *Haunted*
Horde - *A tribe*

degree, account for the shortcomings of this painfully gleaned tale, which shall be called: THE STORY OF THE CALIPH WHO *ALLEVIATED* HIS CONSCIENCE

Old Jacob Spraggins mixed for himself some Scotch and lithia water at his $1,200 oak sideboard. Inspiration must have resulted from its *imbibition*, for immediately afterward he struck the quartered oak soundly with his fist and shouted to the empty dining room:

"By the coke ovens of hell, it must be that ten thousand dollars! If I can get that squared, it'll do the trick."

Thus, by the commonest *artifice* of the trade, having gained your interest, the action of the story will now be suspended, leaving you *grumpily* to consider a sort of dull biography beginning fifteen years before.

When old Jacob was young Jacob he was a breaker boy in a Pennsylvania coal mine. I don't know what a breaker boy is; but his occupation seems to be standing by a coal dump with a wan look and a dinner-pail to have his picture taken for magazine articles. Anyhow, Jacob was one. But, instead of dying of overwork at nine, and leaving his helpless parents and brothers at the mercy of the union strikers' reserve fund, he hitched up his *galluses*, put a dollar or two in a side proposition now and then, and at forty-five was worth $20,000,000.

There now! it's over. Hardly had time to *yawn*, did you? I've seen biographies that - but let us *dissemble*.

I want you to consider Jacob Spraggins, Esq., after he had arrived at the seventh stage of his career. The stages meant are, first, humble origin; second, deserved promotion; third, stockholder; fourth, capitalist; fifth, trust magnate; sixth, rich malefactor; seventh, caliph; eighth, x. The eighth stage shall be left to the higher mathematics.

At fifty-five Jacob retired from active business. The income of a czar was still rolling in on him from coal, iron, real estate, oil, railroads, manufactures, and corporations, but none of it touched Jacob's hands in a raw state. It was a *sterilized increment*, carefully cleaned and dusted and fumigated until it arrived at its ultimate stage of untainted, spotless checks in the white fingers of his private secretary. Jacob built a three-million-dollar palace on a corner lot fronting

Aleviated - *Raised*
Imbibition - *The absorption of solvent by a get*
Artifice - *A clever trick*
Grumpily - *Discontentedly*
Dissemble - *To open wide like a mouth*
Increment - *Something added*

on Nabob Avenue, city of New Bagdad, and began to feel the mantle of the late H. A. Rashid descending upon him. Eventually, Jacob slipped the mantle under his collar, tied it in a neat four-in-hand, and became a licensed *harrier* of our Mesopotamian *proletariat*.

When a man's income becomes so large that the butcher actually sends him the kind of steak he orders, he begins to think about his soul's salvation. Now, the various stages or classes of rich men must not be forgotten. The capitalist can tell you to a dollar the amount of his wealth. The trust *magnate* "estimates" it. The rich malefactor hands you a cigar and denies that he has bought the P. D. & Q. The caliph merely smiles and talks about Hammerstein and the musical *lasses*.

There is a record of tremendous altercation at breakfast in a "Where-to-Dine-Well" tavern between a magnate and his wife, the rift within the loot being that the wife calculated their fortune at a figure $3,000,000 higher than did her future *divorce*. Oh, well, I, myself, heard a similar quarrel between a man and his wife because he found fifty cents less in his pockets than he thought he had. After all, we are all human - Count Tolstoi, R. Fitzsimmons, Peter Pan, and the rest of us.

Don't lose heart because the story seems to be *degenerating* into a sort of moral essay for intellectual readers.

There will be dialogue and stage business pretty soon.

When Jacob first began to compare the eyes of needles with the camels in the Zoo he decided upon organized charity. He had his secretary send a check for one million to the Universal Benevolent Association of the Globe. You may have looked down through a *grating* in front of a decayed warehouse for a nickel that you had dropped through. But that is neither here nor there. The Association acknowledged receipt of his favor of the 24th ult. with enclosure as stated.

Separated by a double line, but still mighty close to the matter under the caption of "Oddities of the Day's News" in an evening paper, Jacob Spraggins read that one "Jasper Spargyous" had "donated $100,000 to the U. B. A. of G." A camel may have a stomach for each day in the week; but I dare not *venture* to accord him whiskers, for fear of the Great Displeasure at Washington; but if he have whiskers, surely not one of them will seem to have been inserted in the

Harrier - *Medium-sized hounds*
Proletariat - *A class of wage earners*
Magnate - *A person of great influence*
Lasses - *Young women*
Degenerating - *Decaying*
Grating - *Imitating*
Venture - *Furnished with*

eye of a needle by that effort of that rich man to enter the K. of H. The right is reserved to reject any and all bids; signed, S. Peter, secretary and gatekeeper.

Next, Jacob selected the best *endowed* college he could scare up and presented it with a $200,000 laboratory. The college did not maintain a scientific course, but it accepted the money and built an elaborate *lavatory* instead, which was no *diversion* of funds so far as Jacob ever discovered.

The faculty met and invited Jacob to come over and take his A B C degree. Before sending the invitation they smiled, cut out the C, added the proper punctuation marks, and all was well.

While walking on the campus before being capped and *gowned*, Jacob saw two professors strolling nearby. Their voices, long adapted to indoor *acoustics*, undesignedly reached his ear.

"There goes the latest *chevalier d'industrie*," said one of them, "to buy a sleeping powder from us. He gets his degree to-morrow."

"*In foro conscientai*," said the other. "Let's 'eave 'arf a brick at 'im."

Jacob ignored the Latin, but the brick pleasantry was not too hard for him. There was no *mandragora* in the honourary draught of learning that he had bought. That was before the passage of the Pure Food and Drugs Act.

Jacob wearied of philanthropy on a large scale.

"If I could see folks made happier," he said to himself - "If I could see 'em myself and hear 'em express their gratitude for what I done for 'em it would make me feel better. This donatin' funds to institutions and societies is about as satisfactory as dropping money into a broken slot machine."

So Jacob followed his nose, which led him through unswept streets to the homes of the poorest. "The very thing!" said Jacob. "I will charter two river steamboats, pack them full of these unfortunate children and - say ten thousand dolls and drums and a thousand freezers of ice cream, and give them a delightful outing up the Sound. The sea breezes on that trip ought to blow the *taint* off some of this money that keeps coming in faster than I can work it off my mind."

Lavatory - *A flush toilet*
Gowned - *To dress in a gown*
Acoustics - *Related to the sense of hearing*
Mandragora - *A eurasian plant*
Taint - *A trade fo something too*

Jacob must have leaked some of his ***benevolent intentions***, for an immense person with a bald face and a mouth that looked as if it ought to have a "Drop Letters Here" sign over it hooked a finger around him and set him in a space between a barber's pole and a stack of ash cans. Words came out of the post-office slit - smooth, husky words with gloves on 'em, but sounding as if they might turn to bare knuckles any moment.

"Say, Sport, do you know where you are at? Well, dis is Mike O'Grady's district you're buttin' into - see? Mike's got de stomach-ache privilege for every kid in dis neighbourhood - see? And if dere's any picnics or red balloons to be dealt out here, Mike's money pays for 'em - see? Don't you butt in, or something'll be handed to you. Youse d - - settlers and reformers with your ***social ologies*** and your millionaire detectives have got dis district in a hell of a fix, anyhow. With your college students and professors rough-housing de soda-water stands and dem rubber-neck coaches fillin' de streets, de folks down here are 'fraid to go out of de houses. Now, you leave 'em to Mike. Dey belongs to him, and he knows how to handle 'em. Keep on your own side of de town. Are you some wiser now, uncle, or do you want to scrap wit' Mike O'Grady for de Santa Claus belt in dis district?"

Clearly, that spot in the moral vineyard was ***preempted***. So Caliph Spraggins menaced no more the people in the bazaars of the East Side. To keep down his growing surplus he doubled his donations to organised charity, presented the Y. M. C. A. of his native town with a $10,000 collection of butterflies, and sent a check to the famine sufferers in China big enough to buy new emerald eyes and diamond-filled teeth for all their gods. But none of these charitable acts seemed to bring peace to the caliph's heart.

He tried to get a personal note into his ***benefactions*** by tipping bellboys and waiters $10 and $20 bills. He got well snickered at and derided for that by the minions who accept with respect gratuities ***commensurate*** to the service performed. He sought out an ambitious and talented but poor young woman, and bought for her the star part in a new comedy. He might have gotten rid of $50,000 more of his ***cumbersome*** money in this philanthropy if he had not neglected to

Preempted - *To acquire before someone else*
Benefaction - *The act of doing good*
Commensurate - *Proportionate, adequate*
Cumbersome - *Troublesome*

write letters to her. But she lost the suit for lack of evidence, while his capital still kept piling up, and his *optikos needleorum camelibus* - or rich man's disease - was unrelieved.

In Caliph Spraggins's $3,000,000 home lived his sister Henrietta, who used to cook for the coal miners in a twenty-five-cent eating house in Coketown, Pa., and who now would have offered John Mitchell only two fingers of her hand to shake. And his daughter Celia, nineteen, back from boarding-school and from being polished off by private instructors in the restaurant languages and those 'etudes and things.

Celia is the heroine. Lest the artist's **delineation** of her charms on this very page humbug your fancy, take from me her authorised description. She was a nice-looking, awkward, loud, rather bashful, brown-haired girl, with a sallow complexion, bright eyes, and a perpetual smile. She had a wholesome, Spraggins-inherited love for plain food, loose clothing, and the society of the lower classes. She had too much health and youth to feel the burden of wealth. She had a wide mouth that kept the peppermint-pepsin tablets rattling like hail from the slot-machine wherever she went, and she could whistle hornpipes. Keep this picture in mind; and let the artist do his worst.

Celia looked out of her window one day and gave her heart to the ***grocer's*** young man. The receiver thereof was at that moment engaged in conceding ***immortality*** to his horse and calling down upon him the ultimate fate of the wicked; so he did not notice the transfer. A horse should stand still when you are lifting a crate of strictly new-laid eggs out of the wagon.

Young lady reader, you would have liked that grocer's young man yourself. But you wouldn't have given him your heart, because you are saving it for a riding-master, or a shoe-manufacturer with a torpid liver, or something quiet but rich in gray tweeds at Palm Beach. Oh, I know about it. So I am glad the grocer's young man was for Celia, and not for you.

The grocer's young man was slim and straight and as confident and easy in his movements as the man in the back of the magazines who wears the new frictionless roller suspenders. He wore a gray bicycle cap on the back of his head, and his hair was straw-coloured and curly, and his

Delineation - *Description*
Everlasting - *Forever*
Wagon - *Four-wheeled*
Contemptuous - *Sneering*

sunburned face looked like one that smiled a good deal when he was not preaching the doctrine of ***everlasting*** punishment to delivery-wagon horses. He slung imported A1 fancy groceries about as though they were only the stuff he delivered at boarding-houses; and when he picked up his whip, your mind instantly recalled Mr. Tacktt and his air with the buttonless foils.

Tradesmen delivered their goods at a side gate at the rear of the house. The grocer's ***wagon*** came about ten in the morning. For three days Celia watched the driver when he came, finding something new each time to admire in the lofty and almost ***contemptuous*** way he had of tossing around the choicest gifts of Pomona, Ceres, and the ***canning*** factories. Then she consulted Annette.

To be ***explicit***, Annette McCorkle, the second housemaid who deserves a paragraph herself. Annette Fletcherized large numbers of romantic novels which she obtained at a free public library branch (donated by one of the biggest caliphs in the business). She was Celia's sidekicker and chum, though Aunt Henrietta didn't know it, you may hazard a bean or two.

"Oh, canary-bird seed!" exclaimed Annette. "Ain't it a corkin' situation? You a heiress, and fallin' in love with him on sight! He's a sweet boy, too, and above his business. But he ain't ***susceptible*** like the common run of grocer's assistants. He never pays no attention to me."

"He will to me," said Celia.

"Riches -" began Annette, unsheathing the not unjustifiable feminine sting.

"Oh, you're not so beautiful," said Celia, with her wide, ***disarming*** smile. "Neither am I; but he sha'n't know that there's any money mixed up with my looks, such as they are. That's fair. Now, I want you to lend me one of your caps and an apron, Annette."

"Oh, marshmallows!" cried Annette. "I see. Ain't it lovely? It's just like 'Lurline, the Left-Handed; or, A Buttonhole Maker's Wrongs.' I'll bet he'll turn out to be a count."

There was a long hallway (or "passageway," as they call it in the land of the Colonels) with one side latticed, running along the rear of the house. The grocer's young man went through this to deliver his goods. One morning he passed a

---

Canning - *The act or process of preserving cooked food*
Explicit - *Clearly develped*
Susceptible - *Capable of being affected*
Disarming - *Winsome, engaging*
Cumbered - *Hindered*
Piccolos - *A small flute*

girl in there with shining eyes, sallow complexion, and wide, smiling mouth, wearing a maid's cap and apron. But as he was *cumbered* with a basket of Early Drumhead lettuce and Trophy tomatoes and three bunches of asparagus and six bottles of the most expensive Queen olives, he saw no more than that she was one of the maids.

But on his way out he came up behind her, and she was whistling "Fisher's Hornpipe" so loudly and clearly that all the *piccolos* in the world should have *disjointed* themselves and crept into their cases for shame.

The grocer's young man stopped and pushed back his cap until it hung on his collar button behind.

"That's out o' sight, Kid," said he.

"My name is Celia, if you please," said the *whistler*, dazzling him with a three-inch smile.

That's all right. I'm Thomas McLeod. What part of the house do you work in?"

"I'm the - the second parlor maid."

"Do you know the 'Falling Waters'?"

"No," said Celia, "we don't know anybody. We got rich too quick - that is, Mr. Spraggins did." "I'll make you *acquainted*," said Thomas McLeod. "It's a strathspey - the first cousin to a hornpipe." If Celia's whistling put the piccolos out of commission, Thomas McLeod's surely made the biggest flutes hunt their holes. He could actually whistle *bass*.

When he stopped Celia was ready to jump into his delivery wagon and ride with him clear to the end of the pier and on to the ferry-boat of the Charon line.

"I'll be around to-morrow at 10:15," said Thomas, "with some spinach and a case of carbonic." "I'll practice that what-you-may-call-it," said Celia. "I can whistle a fine second."

The processes of courtship are personal, and do not belong to general literature. They should be chronicled in detail only in advertisements of iron tonics and in the secret by-laws of the Woman's Auxiliary of the Ancient Order of the Rat Trap. But *genteel* writing may contain a description of certain stages of its progress without intruding upon the province of the X-ray or of park policemen.

Whistler - *A person thing*
Acquainted - *Familar refined*
Genteel - *Well-breet*
Latticed - *Furnished*
Invincible - *Incapable of being conquered defeated*

A day came when Thomas McLeod and Celia lingered at the end of the *latticed* "passage." "Sixteen a week isn't much," said Thomas, letting his cap rest on his shoulder blades.

Celia looked through the lattice-work and whistled a dead march. Shopping with Aunt Henrietta the day before, she had paid that much for a dozen handkerchiefs.

"Maybe I'll get a raise next month," said Thomas. "I'll be around to-morrow at the same time with a bag of flour and the laundry soap."

"All right," said Celia. "Annette's married cousin pays only $20 a month for a flat in the Bronx." Never for a moment did she count on the Spraggins money. She knew Aunt Henrietta's *invincible* pride of caste and pa's mightiness as a Colossus of cash, and she understood that if she chose Thomas she and her grocer's young man might go whistle for a living.

Another day came, Thomas violating the dignity of Nabob Avenue with "The Devil's Dream," whistled keenly between his teeth.

"Raised to eighteen a week yesterday," he said. "Been pricing flats around Morningside. You want to start untying those *apron* strings and *unpinning* that cap, old girl."

"Oh, Tommy!" said Celia, with her broadest smile. "Won't that be enough? I got Betty to show me how to make a cottage pudding. I guess we could call it a flat *pudding* if we wanted to."

"And tell no lie," said Thomas.

"And I can sweep and polish and dust - of course, a parlour maid learns that. And we cold whistle duets of evenings."

"The old man said he'd raise me to twenty at Christmas if Bryan couldn't think of any harder name to call a Republican than a '*postponer*,'" said the grocer's young man.

"I can sew," said Celia; "and I know that you must make the gas company's man show his badge when he comes to look at the meter; and I know how to put up *quince* jam and window curtains."

"Bully! you're all right, Cele. Yes, I believe we can pull it off on eighteen."

Unpinning - *To remove pins from*
Pudding - *A thick, soft dessert*
Postponer - *To put off to a later time*
Quince - *A small widely cultivated Asian rosaceous tree*

As he was jumping into the wagon the second parlor maid braved discovery by running swiftly to the gate.

"And, oh, Tommy, I forgot," she called, softly. "I believe I could make your neckties."

"Forget it," said Thomas decisively.

"And another thing," she continued. "Sliced cucumbers at night will drive away cockroaches." "And sleep, too, you bet," said Mr. McLeod. "Yes, I believe if I have a delivery to make on the West Side this afternoon I'll look in at a furniture store I know over there."

It was just as the wagon dashed away that old Jacob Spraggins struck the sideboard with his fist and made the mysterious remark about ten thousand dollars that you perhaps remember. Which justifies the reflection that some stories, as well as life, and puppies thrown into wells, move around in circles. Painfully but briefly we must shed light on Jacob's words.

The foundation of his fortune was made when he was twenty. A poor coal-digger (ever hear of a rich one?) had saved a dollar or two and bought a small tract of land on a hillside on which he tried to raise corn. Not a ***nubbin***. Jacob, whose nose was a divining-rod, told him there was a vein of coal beneath. he bought the land from the miner for $125 and sold it a month afterward for $10,000. Luckily the miner had enough left of his sale money to drink himself into a black coat opening in the back, as soon as he heard the news.

And so, for forty years afterward, we find Jacob illuminated with the sudden thought that if he could make restitution of this sum of money to the heirs or assigns of the unlucky miner, ***respite*** and Nepenthe might be his.

And now must come swift action, for we have here some four thousand words and not a tear shed and never a pistol, joke, safe, nor bottle cracked.

Old Jacob hired a dozen private detectives to find the heirs, if any existed, of the old miner, Hugh McLeod.

Get the point? Of course I know as well as you do that Thomas is going to be the heir. I might have concealed the name; but why always hold back you mystery till the end?

Nubbin - *A small lump*
Respite -*Temporary relief*
Restitution - *Restoration of property*

I say, let it come near the middle so people can stop reading there if they want to.

After the detectives had trailed false clues about three thousand dollars - I mean miles - they cornered Thomas at the grocery and got his confession that Hugh McLeod had been his grandfather, and that there were no other heirs. They arranged a meeting for him and old Jacob one morning in one of their offices.

Jacob liked the young man very much. He liked the way he looked straight at him when he talked, and the way he threw his bicycle cap over the top of a rose-colored vase on the centre-table. There was a slight flaw in Jacob's system of ***restitution***. He did not consider that the act, to be perfect, should include confession. So he represented himself to be the agent of the purchaser of the land who had sent him to refund the sale price for the ease of his conscience.

"Well, sir," said Thomas, "this sounds to me like an illustrated post-card from South Boston with 'We're having a good time here' written on it. I don't know the game. Is this ten thousand dollars money, or do I have to save so many coupons to get it?"

Old Jacob counted out to him twenty five-hundred-dollar bills.

That was better, he thought, than a check. Thomas put them thoughtfully into his pocket.

"Grandfather's best thanks," he said, "to the party who sends it."

Jacob talked on, asking him about his work, how he spent his ***leisure*** time, and what his ambitions were. The more he saw and heard of Thomas, the better he liked him. He had not met many young men in Bagdad so frank and wholesome.

"I would like to have you visit my house," he said. "I might help you in ***investing*** or laying out your money. I am a very wealthy man. I have a daughter about grown, and I would like for you to know her. There are not many young men I would care to have call on her."

Leisure - *Free or unoccupied*
Estate - *A piece of landed property*
Investing - *To put money to use, by purchase*

"I'm obliged," said Thomas. "I'm not much at making calls. It's generally the side entrance for mine. And, besides, I'm engaged to a girl that has the Delaware peach crop killed in the blossom. She's a parlor maid in a house where I deliver goods. She won't be working there much longer, though. Say, don't forget to give your friend my grandfather's best regards. You'll excuse me now; my wagon's outside with a lot of green stuff that's got to be delivered. See you again, sir."

At eleven Thomas delivered some bunches of parsley and lettuce at the Spraggins mansion. Thomas was only twenty-two; so, as he came back, he took out the handful of five-hundred-dollar bills and waved them carelessly. Annette took a pair of eyes as big as creamed onion to the cook.

"I told you he was a count," she said, after relating. "He never would carry on with me."

"But you say he showed money," said the cook.

"Hundreds of thousands," said Annette. "Carried around loose in his pockets. And he never would look at me."

"It was paid to me to-day," Thomas was explaining to Celia outside. "It came from my grandfather's *estate*. Say, Cele, what's the use of waiting now? I'm going to quit the job to-night. Why can't we get married next week?"

"Tommy," said Celia. "I'm no parlor maid. I've been fooling you. I'm Miss Spraggins - Celia Spraggins. The newspapers say I'll be worth forty million dollars some day."

Thomas pulled his cap down straight on his head for the first time since we have known him. "I suppose then," said he, "I suppose then you'll not be marrying me next week. But you *can* whistle."

"No," said Celia, "I'll not be marrying you next week. My father would never let me marry a grocer's clerk. But I'll marry you to-night, Tommy, if you say so."

Old Jacob Spraggins came home at 9:30 P. M., in his motor car. The make of it you will have to surmise sorrowfully; I am giving you *unsubsidized* fiction; had it been a street car I could have told you its *voltage* and the number of wheels it had. Jacob called for his daughter; he had bought a ruby necklace for her, and wanted to hear her say what a kind, thoughtful, dear old dad he was.

Voltage - *An electromotive force/ potential difference expressed in volts*
Unsubsidized - *No aids*
Remorseful - *Regretful*
Histrionics - *Dramatic representations*

There was a brief search in the house for her, and then came Annette, glowing with the pure flame of truth and loyalty well mixed with envy and *histrionics*.

"Oh, sir," said she, wondering if she should kneel, "Miss Celia's just this minute running away out of the side gate with a young man to be married. I couldn't stop her, sir. They went in a cab."

"What young man?" roared old Jacob.

"A millionaire, if you please, sir - a rich nobleman in disguise. He carries his money with him, and the red peppers and the onions was only to blind us, sir. He never did seem to take to me."

Jacob rushed out in time to catch his car. The chauffeur had been delayed by trying to light a cigarette in the wind.

"Here, Gaston, or Mike, or whatever you call yourself, scoot around the corner quicker than *blazes* and see if you can see a cab. If you do, run it down."

There was a cab in sight a block away. Gaston, or Mike, with his eyes half shut and his mind on his cigarette, picked up the trail, neatly crowded the cab to the curb and pocketed it. "What t'ell you doin'?" yelled the cabman.

"Pa!" shrieked Celia.

"Grandfather's *remorseful* friend's agent!" said Thomas. "Wonder what's on his conscience now."

"A thousand thunders," said Gaston, or Mike. "I have no other match."

"Young man," said old Jacob, severely, "how about that parlor maid you were engaged to?" A couple of years afterward old Jacob went into the office of his private secretary.

"The Amalgamated Missionary Society solicits a contribution of $30,000 toward the conversion of the Koreans," said the secretary.

"Pass 'em up," said Jacob.

"The University of Plumville writes that its yearly *endowment* fund of $50,000 that you bestowed upon it is past due."

"Tell 'em it's been cut out."

"The Scientific Society of Clam Cove, Long Island, asks for $10,000 to buy alcohol to preserve specimens."

Solicits - *To seek for by entreaty, earnest*
Endowment - *Gifts*
Scrubwoman - *A woman hired to clean a place*

"Waste basket."

"The Society for Providing Healthful Recreation for Working Girls wants $20,000 from you to lay out a golf course."

"Tell 'em to see an undertaker."

"Cut 'em all out," went on Jacob. "I've quit being a good thing. I need every dollar I can scrape or save. I want you to write to the directors of every company that I'm interested in and recommend a 10 per cent. cut in salaries. And say - I noticed half a cake of soap lying in a corner of the hall as I came in. I want you to speak to the *scrubwoman* about waste. I've got no money to throw away. And say - we've got vinegar pretty well in hand, haven't we?'

"The Globe Spice & Seasons Company," said secretary, "controls the market at present."

"Raise vinegar two cents a gallon. Notify all our branches."

Suddenly Jacob Spraggin's plump red face relaxed into a pulpy grin. He walked over to the secretary's desk and showed a small red mark on his thick forefinger.

"Bit it," he said, "darned if he didn't, and he ain't had the tooth three weeks - Jaky McLeod, my Celia's kid. He'll be worth a hundred millions by the time he's twenty-one if I can pile it up for him."

As he was leaving, old Jacob turned at the door, and said:

"Better make that *vinegar* raise three cents instead of two. I'll be back in an hour and sign the letters."

The true history of the Caliph Harun Al Rashid relates that toward, the end of his reign he wearied of *philanthropy*, and caused to be *beheaded* all his former favorites and companions of his "Arabian Nights" *rambles*. Happy are we in these days of enlightenment, when the only death warrant the caliphs can serve on us is in the form of a tradesman's bill.

Philanthropy - *The practice of performing charitable actions*
Vinegar - *A sour liquid consisting*
Beheaded - *To cut off the head of*
Rambles - *To wander in an aimless manner*
Warrant - *Authorization*

Food For Thought

Celia plans to elope with Tom Mcleod. Spraggins follows her and is happy that his daughter has chosen Tom Mcleod. What happens a year later ofter Celia's marriage? Why does the author say that Spraggins never really changed? What does he do to amass a fortune for his grandson? Do you think that wealthy people like Spraggins never change and are always after money? Give one example other than this story.

An Understanding

Q. 1. When and where is the story written by O.Henry? What is the setting of the story and why does the millionaire, Jacob Spraggins feeling guilty?
Ans. _____
_____
_____
_____

Q. 2. What does Spraggins do to relieve himself from the feeling of guilt that he had committed years ago?
Ans. _____
_____
_____
_____

Q. 3. Who is McLeod? What happened between Spraggins and McLeod many years ago? How does Spraggins compensate McLeod's grandson, Tom McLeod and why?
Ans. _____
_____
_____
_____

Q. 4. What was Tom McLeod's profession and how did he impress the millionaire, Spraggins? What did Spraggins want from him, and what was the relationship between Tom McLeod and Spraggins daughter, Celia?
Ans. _____
_____
_____
_____
_____

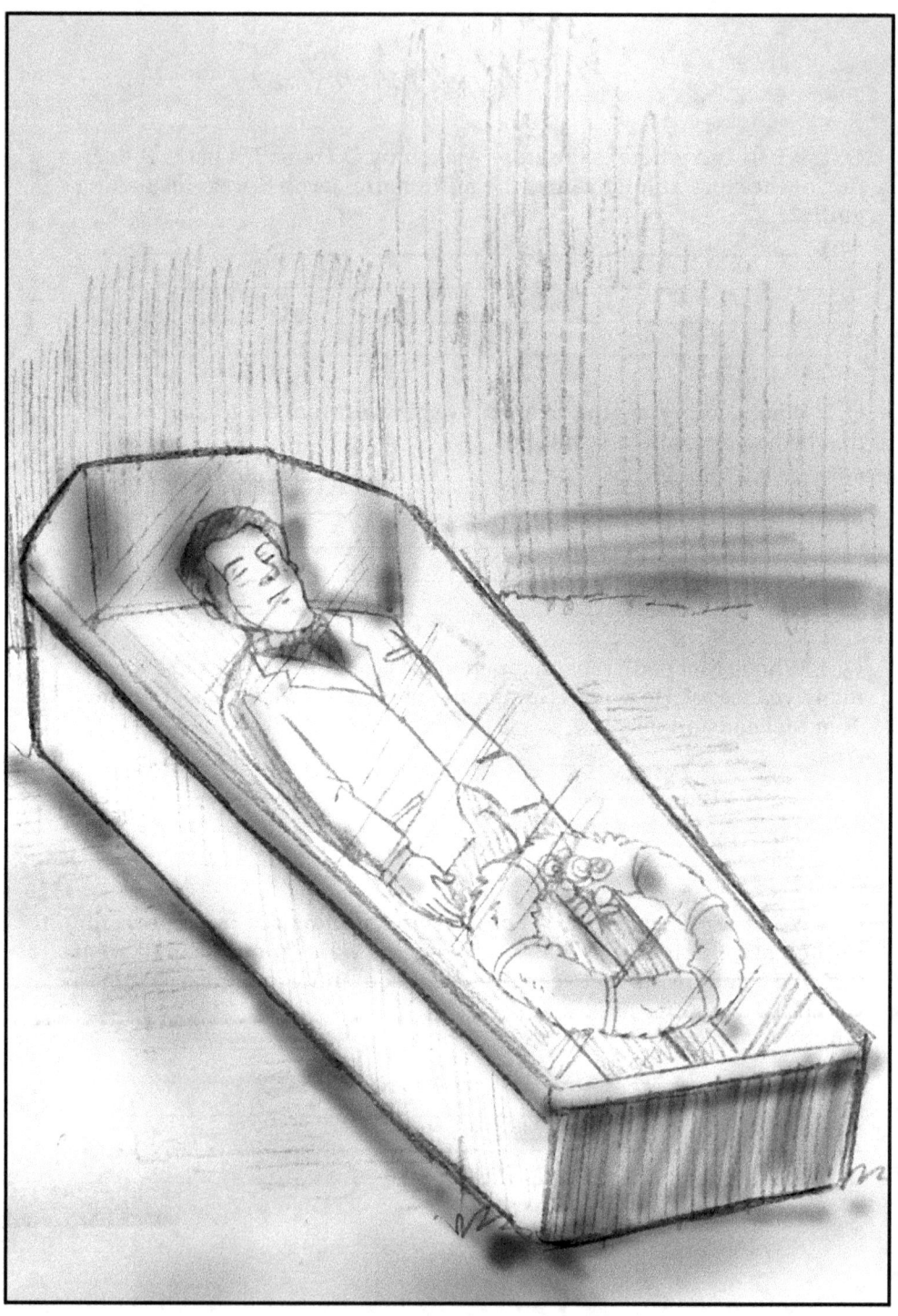

The Baron Of Grogzwig
~ Charles Dickens

THe Baron Von Koëldwethout, of Grogzwig in Germany, was as likely a young baron as you would wish to see. I needn't say that he lived in a castle, because that's of course; neither need I say that he lived in an old castle; for what German baron ever lived in a new one? There were many strange circumstances connected with this venerable building, among which, not the least **startling** and mysterious were, that when the wind blew, it rumbled in the chimneys, or even howled among the trees in the neighbouring forest; and that when the moon shone, she found her way through certain small loopholes in the wall, and actually made some parts of the wide halls and **galleries** quite light, while she left others in gloomy shadow. I believe that one of the baron's ancestors, being short of money, had **inserted** a dagger in a gentleman who called one night to ask his way, and it *was* supposed that these miraculous occurrences took place in **consequence**. And yet I hardly know how that could have been, either, because the baron's ancestor, who was an amiable man, felt very sorry afterwards for having been so rash, and laying violent hands upon a quantity of stone and timber which belonged to a weaker baron, built a **chapel** as an apology, and so took a receipt from Heaven, in full of all demands.

Talking of the baron's ancestor puts me in mind of the baron's great claims to respect, on the score of his pedigree. I am afraid to say, I am sure, how many ancestors the baron had; but I know that he had a great many more than any other man of his time; and I only wish that he had lived in these latter days, that he might have had more. It is a very hard thing upon the great men of past centuries, that they should have come into the world so soon, because a man who was born three or four hundred years ago, cannot reasonably be expected to have had as many relations before him, as a man who is born now. The last man, whoever he is - and he may be a cobbler or some low vulgar dog for aught we know - will have a longer **pedigree** than the greatest nobleman now alive; and I contend that this is not fair.

Chapel - *A private place of prayer*
Startling - *Surprise, wonder*
Galleries - *Rooms*
Inserted - *Attached to*
Consequence - *Result*

Well, but the Baron Von Koëldwethout of Grogzwig! He was a fine *swarthy* fellow, with dark hair and large *moustachios*, who rode a-hunting in clothes of Lincoln green, with russet boots on his feet, and a bugle slung over his shoulder, like the guard of a long stage. When he blew this bugle, four-and-twenty other gentlemen of inferior rank, in Lincoln green a little *coarser*, and russet boots with a little thicker soles, turned out directly; and away galloped the whole train, with spears in their hands like *lackered* area railings, to hunt down the boars, or perhaps *encounter* a bear: in which latter case the baron killed him first, and greased his *whiskers* with him afterwards.

This was a merry life for the Baron of Grogzwig, and a merrier still for the baron's retainers, who drank Rhine wine every night till they fell under the table, and then had the bottles on the floor, and called for pipes. Never were such jolly, roystering, rollicking, merry-making blades, as the jovial crew of Grogzwig.

But the pleasures of the table, or the pleasures of under the table, require a little variety; especially when the same five-and-twenty people sit daily down to the same board, to discuss the same subjects, and tell the same stories. The baron grew weary, and wanted excitement. He took to quarrelling with his gentlemen, and tried kicking two or three of them every day after dinner. This was a pleasant change at first; but it became monotonous after a week or so, and the baron felt quite out of sorts, and cast about, in *despair*, for some new amusement.

One night, after a day's sport in which he had outdone Nimrod or Gillingwater, and *slaughtered* "another fine bear", and brought him home in triumph, the Baron Von Koëldwethout sat moodily at the head of his table, eyeing the smoky roof of the hall with a *discontented* aspect. He swallowed huge bumpers of wine, but the more he swallowed, the more he *frowned*. The gentlemen who had been honoured with the dangerous distinction of sitting on his right and left, imitated him to a miracle in the drinking, and frowned at each other.

"I will!" cried the baron suddenly, smiting the table with his right hand, and twirling his moustache with his left. "Fill to the Lady of Grogzwig!"

Frowned - *To contract the brow*
Encounter - *To come upon or meet with*
Slaughtered - *Butchered*
Swarthy - *Dark*
Moustachios - *Moustache*
Coarser - *Rougher*

The four-and-twenty Lincoln greens turned pale, with the exception of their four-and-twenty noses, which were unchangeable.

"I said to the Lady of Grogzwig," repeated the baron, looking round the board. "To the Lady of Grogzwig!" shouted the Lincoln greens; and down their four-and-twenty throats went four-and-twenty *imperial pints* of such rare old hock, that they *smacked* their eight-and-forty lips, and *winked* again.

"The fair daughter of the Baron Von Swillenhausen," said Koëldwethout, condescending to explain. "We will demand her in marriage of her father, ere the sun goes down tomorrow. If he refuse our suit, we will cut off his nose."

A hoarse murmur arose from the company; every man touched, first the *hilt* of his sword, and then the tip of his nose, with appalling significance.

What a pleasant thing filial piety is, to contemplate! If the daughter of the Baron Von Swillenhausen had pleaded a preoccupied heart, or fallen at her father's feet and corned them in salt tears, or only fainted away, and complimented the old gentleman in frantic *ejaculations*, the odds are a hundred to one, but Swillenhausen castle would have been turned out at window, or rather the baron turned out at window, and the castle demolished. The damsel held her peace, however, when an early messenger bore the request of Von Koëldwethout next morning, and modestly retired to her chamber, from the casement of which she watched the coming of the suitor and his *retinue*. She was no sooner assured that the horseman with the large moustachios was her proffered husband, than she *hastened* to her father's presence, and expressed her readiness to sacrifice herself to secure his peace. The *venerable* baron caught his child into his arms, and shed a wink of joy.

There was a great feasting at the castle, that day. The four-and-twenty Lincoln greens of Von Koëldwethout exchanged vows of *eternal* friendship with twelve Lincoln greens of Von Swillenhausen, and promised the old baron that they would drink his wine "Till all was blue" - meaning probably until their whole countenances had acquired the same tint as their noses. Everybody slapped everybody else's back, when the time for parting came; and the Baron Von Koëldwethout and his followers rode gaily home.

Imperial - *Kingly*
Pints - *Units of liquid measure*
Winked - *To close/open*
Smacked - *A taste*
Hilt - *The handle of as word*
Ejaculations - *An abrupt emphatic utterance*

For six mortal weeks, the bears and boars had a holiday. The houses of Koëldwethout and Swillenhausen were united; the spears *rusted*; and the baron's bugle grew hoarse for lack of blowing.

Those were great times for the four-and-twenty; but, alas! their high and *palmy* days had taken boots to themselves, and were already walking off.

"My dear," said the baroness.

"My love," said the baron.

"Those coarse, noisy men --"

"Which, ma'am?" said the baron starting.

The baroness pointed, from the window at which they stood, to the *courtyard* beneath, where the unconscious Lincoln greens were taking a *copious stirrup-cup,* preparatory to issuing forth, after a boar or two.

"My hunting train, ma'am," said the baron.

"Disband them, love," murmured the baroness.

"*Disband* them!" cried the baron, in amazement.

"To please me, love," replied the baroness.

"To please the devil, ma'am," answered the baron.

Whereupon the baroness uttered a great cry, and *swooned* away at the baron's feet.

What could the baron do? He called for the lady's maid, and roared for the doctor; and then, rushing into the yard, kicked the two Lincoln greens who were the most used to it, and cursing the others all round, bade them go - but never mind where, I don't know the German for it, or I would put it delicately that way.

It is not for me to say by what means or by what degrees, some wives manage to keep down some husbands as they do, although I may have my private opinion on the subject, and may think that no Member of Parliament ought to be married, in as much as three married members out of every four, must vote according to their wives' consciences (if there be such things), and not according to their own. All I need say, just now, is, that the Baroness Von Koëldwethout somehow or other acquired great control over the Baron Von Koëldwethout, and that, little by little, and bit by bit, and day by day, and year by year, the baron got the worst of some disputed question, or was slyly unhorsed from some old hobby; and that by the time he was a fat hearty fellow of forty-eight or *thereabouts*, he had no

Rusted - *A stain*
Palmy - *Glorious*
Courtyard - *An open area*
Copious - *Large quantity*
Stirrup-cup - *Farewell drink*
Disband - *To disperse*
Swooned - *Fainted*

feasting, no revelry, no hunting train, and no hunting - nothing in short that he liked, or used to have; and that, although he was as fierce as a lion and as bold as brass, he was decidedly *snubbed* and put down, by his own lady, in his own castle of Grogzwig.

Nor was this the whole extent of the baron's misfortunes. About a year after his *nuptials*, there came into the world a lusty young baron, in whose honour a great many fireworks were let off, and a great many dozens of wine drunk; but next year there came a young baroness, and next year another young baron, and so on, every year, either a baron or baroness (and one year both together), until the baron found himself the father of a small family of twelve. Upon every one of these anniversaries, the venerable Baroness Von Swillenhausen was nervously sensitive for the well-being of her child the Baroness Von Koëldwethout and although it was not found that the good lady ever did anything material towards contributing to her child's recovery, still she made it a point of duty to be as nervous as possible at the castle at Grogzwig, and to divide her time between moral observations on the baron's housekeeping, and *bewailing* the hard lot of her unhappy daughter. And if the Baron of Grogzwig, a little hurt and irritated at this, took heart, and ventured to suggest that his wife was at least no worse off than the wives of other barons, the Baroness Von Swillenhausen begged all persons to take notice, that nobody but she, sympathised with her dear daughter's sufferings; upon which, her relations and friends remarked, that to be sure she did cry a great deal more than her son-in-law, and that if there were a hard-hearted brute alive, it was that Baron of Grogzwig.

The poor baron bore it all, as long as he could, and when he could bear it no longer lost his appetite and his spirits, and sat himself gloomily and *dejectedly* down. But there were worse troubles yet in store for him, and as they came on, his *melancholy* and sadness increased. Times changed. He got into debt. The Grogzwig coffers ran low, though the Swillenhausen family had looked upon them as *inexhaustible*; and just when the baroness was on the point of making a thirteenth addition to the family pedigree, Von Koëldwethout discovered that he had no means of replenishing them.

"I don't see what is to be done," said the baron. "I think I'll kill myself."

Snubbed - *To check or reject with a sharp rebuke*
Nuptials - *Pertaining to marriage*
Bewailing - *Expressing grief*
Dejectedly - *Depressed*
Melancholy - *Sadness*
Inexhaustible - *Endless*

This was a bright idea. The baron took an old hunting-knife from a cupboard hard by, and having sharpened it on his boot, made what boys call "an offer" at his throat.

"Hem!" said the baron, stopping short. "Perhaps it's not sharp enough."

The baron sharpened it again, and made another offer, when his hand was arrested by a loud screaming among the young barons and baronesses, who had a nursery in an upstairs tower with iron bars outside the window, to prevent their tumbling out into the moat.

"If I had been a bachelor," said the baron sighing, "I might have done it fifty times over, without being interrupted. Hallo! Put a flask of wine and the largest pipe, in the little *vaulted* room behind the hall."

One of the domestics, in a very kind manner, executed the baron's order in the course of half an hour or so, and Von Koëldwethout being *apprised* thereof, strode to the vaulted room, the walls of which, being of dark shining wood, *gleamed* in the light of the *blazing* logs which were piled upon the hearth. The bottle and pipe were ready, and, upon the whole, the place looked very comfortable.

"Leave the lamp," said the baron.

"Anything else, my lord?" inquired the domestic.

"The room," replied the baron. The domestic obeyed, and the baron locked the door.

"I'll smoke a last pipe," said the baron, "and then I'll be off." So, putting the knife upon the table till he wanted it, and *tossing* off a goodly measure of wine, the Lord of Grogzwig threw himself back in his chair, stretched his legs out before the fire, and puffed away.

He thought about a great many things - about his present troubles and past days of bachelorship, and about the Lincoln greens, long since disappeared up and down the country, no one knew whither: with the exception of two who had been unfortunately beheaded, and four who had killed themselves with drinking. His mind was running upon bears and boars, when, in the process of draining his glass to the bottom, he raised his eyes, and saw, for the first time and with unbounded astonishment, that he was not alone.

Vaulted - *An arched structure made of stones resembling a vault*
Apprised - *Informed*
Blazing - *Burning brightly*
Gleamed - *A flash or beam of light*

No, he was not; for, on the opposite side of the fire, there sat with folded arms a **wrinkled hideous** figure, with deeply sunk and bloodshot eyes, and an immensely long, cadaverous face, shadowed by **jagged** and **matted** locks of coarse black hair. He wore a kind of **tunic** of a dull bluish colour, which, the baron observed, on regarding it **attentively**, was clasped or **ornamented** down the front, with coffin handles. His legs too, were **encased** in **coffin** plates as though in armour; and over his left shoulder he wore a short dusky cloak, which seemed made of **remnant** of some pall. He took no notice of the baron, but was intently eyeing the fire.

"Halloa!" said the baron, stamping his foot to attract attention.

"Halloa!" replied the stranger, moving his eyes towards the baron, but not his face or himself. "What now?"

"What now?" replied the baron, nothing daunted by his hollow voice and lustreless eyes, "*I* should ask that question. How did you get here?"

"Through the door," replied the figure.

"What are you?" says the baron.

"A man," replied the figure.

"I don't believe it," says the baron.

"Disbelieve it then," says the figure.

"I will," rejoined the baron.

The figure looked at the bold Baron of Grogzwig for some time, and then said familiarly, "There's no coming over you, I see. I'm not a man!"

"What are you then?" asked the baron.

"A genius," replied the figure.

"You don't look much like one," returned the baron **scornfully**.

"I am the Genius of Despair and Suicide," said the apparition. "Now you know me."

With these words the apparition turned towards the baron, as if composing himself for a talk - and, what was very remarkable, was, that he threw his cloak aside, and displaying a stake, which was run through the centre of his body, pulled it out with a jerk, and laid it on the table, as composedly as if it had been a walking-stick.

"Now," said the figure, glancing at the hunting-knife, "are you ready for me?"

Jagged - *Having a rash, harsh*
Attentively - *Heedful, mindful*
Encased - *Enclose on a case*
Remnant - *Remaining*
Scornfully - *Contemptuously*

"Not quite," rejoined the baron; "I must finish this pipe first."

"Look sharp then," said the figure.

You seem in a hurry," said the baron.

"Why, yes, I am," answered the figure; "they're doing a pretty *brisk* business in my way, over in England and France just now, and my time is a good deal taken up."

"Do you drink?" said the baron, touching the bottle with the bowl of his pipe.

"Nine times out of ten, and then very hard," rejoined the figure, dryly.

"Never in moderation?" asked the baron.

"Never," replied the figure, with a *shudder*, "that breeds cheerfulness."

The baron took another look at his new friend, whom he thought an uncommonly queer customer, and at length inquired whether he took any active part in such little proceedings as that which he had in *contemplation*.

"No," replied the figure *evasively*; "but I am always present."

"Just to see fair, I suppose?" said the baron.

"Just that," replied the figure playing with the stake, and examining the ferule.

"Be as quick as you can, will you, for there's a young gentleman who is afflicted with too much money and leisure wanting me now, I find."

"Going to kill himself because he has too much money!" exclaimed the baron, quite tickled: "Ha! ha! that's a good one." (This was the first time the baron had laughed for many a long day.)

"I say," *expostulated* the figure, looking very much scared; "don't do that again."

"Why not?" demanded the baron.

"Because it gives me pain all over," replied the figure. "Sigh as much as you please; that does me good."

The baron sighed mechanically, at the mention of the word; the figure, brightening up again, handed him the hunting-knife with the most winning politeness.

"It's not a bad idea though," said the baron, feeling the edge of the weapon; "a man killing himself because he has too much money."

"Pooh!" said the apparition, *petulantly*, "no better than a man's killing himself because he has none or little."

Brisk - *Quick, fast*
Shudder - *Shiver, tremble*
Contemplation - *Consideration, meditation*
Evasively - *Avoidingly*
Expostulated - *Disapproval*
Petulantly - *Impatient irritation*

Whether the genius *unintentionally committed* himself in saying this, or whether he thought the baron's mind was so thoroughly made up that it didn't matter what he said, I have no means of knowing. I only know that the baron stopped his hand, all of a sudden, opened his eyes wide, and looked as if quite a new light had come upon him for the first time. "Why, certainly," said Von Koëldwethout, "nothing is too bad to be retrieved."

"Except empty coffers," cried the genius.

"Well, but they may be one day filled again," said the baron.

"Scolding wives," snarled the genius.

"Oh! They may be made quiet," said the baron.

"Thirteen children," shouted the genius.

"Can't all go wrong, surely," said the baron.

The genius was *evidently* growing very savage with the baron, for holding these opinions all at once; but he tried to laugh it off, and said if he would let him know when he had left off joking, he should feel obliged to him.

"But I am not joking; I was never farther from it," remonstrated the baron.

"Well, I am glad to hear that," said the genius, looking very *grim*, "because a joke, without any figure of speech, *is* the death of me. Come! Quit this *dreary* world at once."

"I don't know," said the baron, playing with the knife; "it's a dreary one certainly, but I don't think yours is much better, for you have not the appearance of being particularly comfortable. That puts me in mind - what security have I, that I shall be any the better for going out of the world after all!" he cried, starting up; "I never thought of that."

"Dispatch," cried the figure, *gnashing* its teeth.

"Keep off!" said the baron, "I'll brood over miseries no longer, but put a good face on the matter, and try the fresh air and the bears again; and if that don't do, I'll talk to the baroness soundly, and cut the Von Swillenhausens dead." With this the baron fell into his chair, and laughed so loud and *boisterously*, that the room rang with it.

The figure fell back a pace or two, regarding the baron meanwhile with a look of intense terror, and when he had ceased, caught up the stake, plunged it violently into its body, uttered a frightful howl, and disappeared.

Unintentionally - *Accidently*
Committed - *To give in trust*
Grim - *Stern, harsh*
Dreary - *Dull boring*
Gnashing - *To grid*

Hipped - *Greatly interested*
Tempted - *Allured, attracted*
Retire - *To withdraw*
Laudable - *Praiseworthy*

Von Koëldwethout never saw it again. Having once made up his mind to action, he soon brought the baroness and the Von Swillenhausens to reason, and died many years afterwards; not a rich man that I am aware of, but certainly a happy one: leaving behind him a numerous family, who had been carefully educated in bear- and boar-hunting under his own personal eye. And my advice to all men is, that if ever they become *hipped* and melancholy from similar causes (as very many men do), they look at both sides of the question, applying a magnifying glass to the best one; and if they still feel *tempted* to *retire* without leave, that they smoke a large pipe and drink a full bottle first, and profit by the *laudable* example of the baron of Grogzwig.

Food For Thought

The Baron, Koeldwethout encounters a ghostly figure who, calls himself, "The Genius of Despair and Suicide." Why do you think that the Baron was unhappy with his life and marriage? Why did he want to commit suicide? What happens at the end of the story? Do you agree with the conclusion and the realisation that life is not something that you quit when things are not going your way? Give reasons for your answer.

An Understanding

Q. 1. Describe the physical appearance and give a brief character sketch of Koeldwethout's. Who was he and to which country did he belong to?
Ans. _____
_____
_____
_____
_____

Q. 2. What was Baron Von Koeldwethout's favourite pastime and how was his life?
Ans. _____
_____
_____
_____
_____

Q. 3. What did Koeldwethout declare one day at dinner? Who was Baron Von Swillenhausen?
Ans. _____
_____
_____
_____
_____

Q. 4. Whom did Koeldwethout marry and how was his married life? What happened later?
Ans. _____
_____
_____
_____
_____

John Mortonson's Funeral
~Ambrose Bierce

John Mortonson was dead: his lines in 'the tragedy "Man"' had all been spoken and he had left the stage.

The body rested in a fine **mahogany** coffin fitted with a plate of glass. All arrangements for the **funeral** had been so well attended to that had the **deceased** known he would doubtless have **approved**. The face, as it showed under the glass, was not **disagreeable** to look upon: it bore a faint smile, and as the death had been painless, had not been **distorted** beyond the repairing power of the undertaker. At two o'clock of the afternoon the friends were to assemble to pay their last tribute of respect to one who had no further need of friends and respect. The surviving members of the family came severally every few minutes to the **casket** and wept above the placid features beneath the glass. This did them no good; it did no good to John Mortonson; but in the presence of death reason and philosophy are silent.

As the hour of two approached, the friends began to arrive and after offering such **consolation** to the stricken relatives as the **proprieties** of the occasion required, solemnly seated themselves about the room with an **augmented** consciousness of their importance in the scheme funereal. Then the minister came, and in that overshadowing presence the lesser lights went into eclipse. His entrance was followed by that of the widow, whose **lamentations** filled the room. She approached the casket and after leaning her face against the cold glass for a moment was gently led to a seat near her daughter. Mournfully and low the man of God began his **eulogy** of the dead, and his doleful voice, mingled with the **sobbing** which it was its purpose to stimulate and sustain, rose and fell, seemed to come and go, like the sound of a sullen sea. The gloomy day grew darker as he spoke; a curtain of cloud underspread the sky and a few drops of rain fell audibly. It seemed as if all nature were weeping for John Mortonson.

When the minister had finished his eulogy with prayer a hymn was sung and the **pall-bearers** took their places beside the bier. As the last notes of the hymn died away the widow ran to the coffin, cast herself upon it and sobbed **hysterically**.

Hysterically - *Uncontrollably emotional*
Casket - *A small chest*
Lamentation - *Expressing grief*
Eulogy - *A speech writing in praise*
Proprieties - *Decency, modesty*
Avgmented - *Enlarge in size*

Gradually, however, she **yielded** to **dissuasion**, becoming more **composed**; and as the minister was in the act of leading her away, her eyes sought the face of the dead beneath the glass. She threw up her arms and with a **shriek** fell backward insensible.

The **mourners** sprang forward to the coffin, the friends followed, and as the clock on the **mantel solemnly** struck three, all were staring down upon the face of John Mortonson, deceased. They turned away, sick and faint. One man, trying in his terror to escape the awful sight, **stumbled** against the coffin so heavily as to knock away one of its frail supports. The coffin fell to the floor, the glass was shattered to bits by the **concussion**.

From the opening crawled John Mortonson's cat, which lazily leapt to the floor, sat up, **tranquilly** wiped its crimson muzzle with a forepaw, then walked with dignity from the room.

Yielded - *To produce, give up*
Dissuasion - *To advise against*
Mourners - *Persons who attend a funeral of a deceased*
Mantel - *A construction of a fireplace*
Concussion - *Injury to the brain*
Tranquilly - *Peacefully*

Food For Thought

John Mortonson's cat had pounced his paws and drank the blood of his own master. What sort of sight do you think it would have been? Why did the cat attack his own master? Do such things happen and have you ever come across any such incident in your life?

An Understanding

Q. 1. John Mortonson was dead and his body was lying in a mahogany coffin fitted with a plate of glass. What were his friends and family members doing? Why does the author feel that mourning before the dead was futile?
Ans. _____

_____
_____
_____
_____

Q. 2. Who followed the minister and what did she do? Why does the author feel that nature too was weeping for John Mortonson?
Ans. _____

_____
_____
_____
_____

Q. 3. What formalities did the minister perform followed by the pall - bearers? What happened next and why did John Mortonson's wife shriek and fall backwards insensibly?
Ans. _____

_____
_____
_____
_____

Q. 4. Why did the mourners spring forward towards the coffin and then turned away, sick and faint? What had happened suddenly?
Ans. _____

_____
_____
_____
_____

Greatest Humour Stories

The Gold That Glittered
~ O. Henry

A story with a moral appended is like the bill of a mosquito. It bores you, and then injects a stinging drop to *irritate* your *conscience*. Therefore let us have the moral first and be done with it. All is not gold that *glitters*, but it is a wise child that keeps the stopper in his bottle of testing acid.

Where Broadway skirts the corner of the square presided over by George the Veracious is the Little Rialto. Here stand the actors of that quarter, and this is their *shibboleth*: "'Nit,' says I to Frohman, 'you can't touch me for a *kopeck* less than two-fifty per,' and out I walks."

Westward and southward from the Thespian *glare* are one or two streets where a Spanish-American colony has huddled for a little tropical warmth in the *nipping* North. The centre of life in this *precinct* is "El Refugio," a cafe and restaurant that caters to the volatile exiles from the South. Up from Chili, Bolivia, Colombia, the rolling republics of Central America and the ireful islands of the Western Indies flit the cloaked and sombreroed senores, who are scattered like burning lava by the political eruptions of their several countries.

Hither they come to lay counterplots, to bide their time, to solicit funds, to enlist filibusterers, to smuggle out arms and *ammunitions*, to play the game at long taw. In El Refugio, they find the atmosphere in which they thrive.

In the restaurant of El Refugio are served compounds delightful to the palate of the man from Capricorn or Cancer. Altruism must halt the story thus long. On, diner, weary of the *culinary subterfuges* of the Gallic chef, hie thee to El Refugio! There only will you find a fish - bluefish, shad or pompano from the Gulf - baked after the Spanish method. Tomatoes give it color, individuality and soul; chili colorado bestows upon it zest, originality and fervor; unknown herbs furnish *piquancy* and mystery, and - but its crowning glory deserves a new sentence. Around it, above it, beneath it, in its *vicinity* - but never in it - hovers an *ethereal* aura, an *effluvium* so rarefied and delicate that only the Society for Psychical Research could note its origin. Do not say that garlic is in the fish at El Refugio. It is not otherwise than as if the spirit of Garlic, flitting past, has *wafted*

Vicinity - *The area*
Effluvium - *A slight*
Piquancy - *Spicy, sharp*
Subterfuges - *Deception scheme*
Shibboleth - *A slogan*
Precinet - *Encloseed area*

one kiss that *lingers* in the *parsley-crowned* dish as haunting as those kisses in life, "by hopeless fancy feigned on lips that are for others." And then, when Conchito, the waiter, brings you a plate of brown frijoles and carafe of wine that has never stood still between Oporto and El Refugio - ah, Dios!

One day a Hamburg-American liner deposited upon Pier No. 55 Gen. Perrico Ximenes Villablanca Falcon, a passenger from Cartagena. The General was between a claybank and bay in complexion, had a 42-inch waist and stood 5 feet 4 with his Du Barry heels. He had the mustache of a shooting-gallery *proprietor*, he wore the full dress of a Texas congressman and had the important aspect of an uninstructed delegate.

Gen. Falcon had enough English under his hat to enable him to inquire his way to the street in which El Refugio stood. When he reached that neighbourhood he saw a sign before a respectable red-brick house that read, "Hotel Espanol." In the window was a card in Spanish, "Aqui se habla Espanol." The General entered, sure of a congenial port.

In the cozy office was Mrs. O'Brien, the proprietress. She had blond - oh, *unimpeachably* blond hair. For the rest she was amiability, and ran largely to inches around. Gen. Falcon brushed the floor with his broad-brimmed hat, and emitted a quantity of Spanish, the syllables sounding like firecrackers gently popping their way down the string of a bunch.

"Spanish or Dago?" asked Mrs. O'Brien, pleasantly.

"I am a Colombian, madam," said the General, proudly. "I speak the Spanish. The advisment in your window say the Spanish he is spoken here. How is that?"

"Well, you've been speaking it, ain't you?" said the madam. "I'm sure I can't."

At the Hotel Espanol General Falcon engaged rooms and established himself. At dusk he *sauntered* out upon the streets to view the wonders of this roaring city of the North. As he walked he thought of the wonderful golden hair of Mme. O'Brien. "It is here," said the General to himself, no doubt in his own language, "that one shall find the most beautiful *senoras* in the world. I have not in my Colombia viewed among our beauties one so fair. But no! It is not for the General Falcon to think of beauty. It is my country that claims my devotion." At the corner of Broadway and the Little Rialto the General became involved. The street cars *bewildered* him,

Sauntered - *To walk with a leisurely gait*
Unimpeachably - *Above suspicion*
Wafted - *To remain*

and the *fender* of one upset him against a pushcart laden with oranges. A cab driver missed him an inch with a hub, and poured barbarous execrations upon his head. He *scrambled* to the *sidewalk* and skipped again in terror when the whistle of a peanut-roaster puffed a hot scream in his ear. V'algame Dios! What devil's city is this?"

As the General fluttered out of the streamers of passers like a wounded snipe he was marked simultaneously as game by two hunters. One was "Bully" McGuire, whose system of sport required the use of a strong arm and the misuse of an eight-inch piece of lead pipe. The other Nimrod of the asphalt was "Spider" Kelley, a sportsman with more refined methods.

In pouncing upon their self-evident prey, Mr. Kelley was a shade the quicker. His elbow fended accurately the onslaught of Mr. McGuire.

"G'wan!" he commanded harshly. "I saw it first." McGuire *slunk* away, awed by superior intelligence. "Pardon me," said Mr. Kelley, to the General, "but you got balled up in the shuffle, didn't you? Let me assist you." He picked up the General's hat and brushed the dust from it.

The ways of Mr. Kelley could not but succeed. The General, bewildered and **dismayed** by the resounding streets, welcomed his deliverer as a *caballero* with a most disinterested heart. "I have a desire," said the General, "to return to the hotel of O'Brien, in which I am stop. Caramba! senor, there is a loudness and rapidness of going and coming in the city of this Nueva York."

Mr. Kelley's politeness would not suffer the distinguished Colombian to brave the dangers of the return unaccompanied. At the door of the Hotel Espanol they paused. A little lower down on the opposite side of the street shone the modest illuminated sign of El Refugio. Mr. Kelley, to whom few streets were unfamiliar, knew the place exteriorly as a "Dago joint." All foreigners, Mr. Kelley classed under the two heads of "Dagoes" and Frenchmen. He proposed to the General that they repair thither and *substantiate* their acquaintance with a liquid foundation.

An hour later found General Falcon and Mr. Kelley seated at a table in the conspirator's corner of El Refugio. Bottles and glasses were between them. For the tenth time the General confided the secret of his mission to the Estados Unidos. He

Fender - *A device on the front of a locomotive*
Slunk - *To move*
Caballero - *A spanish gentle man*
Substantiate - *Schemer*

was here, he declared, to purchase arms - 2,000 stands of Winchester rifles - for the Colombian revolutionists. He had drafts in his pocket drawn by the Cartagena Bank on its New York *correspondent* for $25,000. At other tables other revolutionists were shouting their political secrets to their fellow-plotters; but none was as loud as the General. He *pounded* the table; he hallooed for some wine; he roared to his friend that his *errand* was a secret one, and not to be hinted at to a living soul. Mr. Kelley himself was *stirred* to sympathetic *enthusiasm*. He grasped the General's hand across the table.

"Monseer," he said, *earnestly*, "I don't know where this country of yours is, but I'm for it. I guess it must be a branch of the United States, though, for the poetry guys and the schoolmarms call us Columbia, too, sometimes. It's a lucky thing for you that you butted into me to-night. I'm the only man in New York that can get this gun deal through for you. The Secretary of War of the United States is me best friend. He's in the city now, and I'll see him for you to-morrow. In the meantime, *monseer*, you keep them drafts tight in your inside pocket. I'll call for you to-morrow, and take you to see him. Say! that ain't the District of Columbia you're talking about, is it?" concluded Mr. Kelley, with a sudden *qualm*. "You can't capture that with no 2,000 guns - it's been tried with more."

"No, no, no!" exclaimed the General. "It is the Republic of Colombia - it is a g-r-reat republic on the top side of America of the South. Yes. Yes."

"All right," said Mr. Kelley, reassured. "Now suppose we trek along home and go by-by. I'll write to the Secretary to-night and make a date with him. It's a *ticklish* job to get guns out of New York. McClusky himself can't do it."

They parted at the door of the Hotel Espanol. The General rolled his eyes at the moon and sighed. "It is a great country, your Nueva York," he said. "Truly the cars in the streets devastate one, and the engine that cooks the nuts terribly makes a *squeak* in the ear. But, ah, Senor Kelley - the senoras with hair of much goldness, and admirable fatness - they are *magnificas*! Muy magnificas!"

Kelley went to the nearest telephone booth and called up McCrary's cafe, far up on Broadway. He asked for Jimmy Dunn.

"Is that Jimmy Dunn?" asked Kelley.

Errand - *A short and quick tip for a specific purpose*
Monieur - *A french title*
Qualm - *An uneasy feeling*
Ticklish - *Extremely sensitive*
Magnificas *-Magnificent*

"Yes," came the answer.

"You're a liar," sang back Kelley, joyfully. "Your'e the Secretary of War. Wait there till I come up. I've got the finest thing down here in the way of a fish you ever baited for. It's a Colorado-maduro, with a gold band around it and free coupons enough to buy a red hall lamp and a statuette of Psyche rubbering in the brook. I'll be up on the next car."

Jimmy Dunn was an A. M. of Crookdom. He was an artist in the confidence line. He never saw a bludgeon in his life; and he scorned knockout drops. In fact, he would have set nothing before an intended victim but the purest of drinks, if it had been possible to procure such a thing in New York. It was the ambition of "Spider" Kelley to elevate himself into Jimmy's class.

These two gentlemen held a conference that night at McCrary's. Kelley explained.

"He's as easy as a gumshoe. He's from the Island of Colombia, where there's a strike, or a feud, or something going on, and they've sent him up here to buy 2,000 Winchesters to *arbitrate* the thing with. He showed me two drafts for $10,000 each, and one for $5,000 on a bank here. 'S truth, Jimmy, I felt real mad with him because he didn't have it in thousand-dollar bills, and hand it to me on a silver waiter. Now, we've got to wait till he goes to the bank and gets the money for us."

They talked it over for two hours, and then Dunn said; "Bring him to No. __ Broadway, at four o'clock to-morrow afternoon."

In due time Kelley called at the Hotel Espanol for the General. He found the wily warrior engaged in *delectable* conversation with Mrs. O'Brien.

"The Secretary of War is waitin' for us," said Kelley.

The General tore himself away with an effort.

"Ay, *senor*," he said, with a sigh, "duty makes a call. But, senor, the senoras of your Estados Unidos - how beauties! For *exemplification*, take you la Madame O'Brien - que magnifica! She is one goddess - one Juno - what you call one ox-eyed Juno."

Now Mr. Kelley was a wit; and better men have been shrivelled by the fire of their own imagination. "Sure!" he said with a grin; "but you mean a peroxide Juno, don't you?"

Arbitrate - *To settle*
Delectable - *Delightful*
Senor - *A spanish-speaking man*
Emplification - *An officially certifiedl copy of a document*

Mrs. O'Brien heard, and lifted an *auriferous* head. Her businesslike eye rested for an instant upon the disappearing form of Mr. Kelley. Except in street cars one should never be unnecessarily *rude* to a lady.

When the *gallant* Colombian and his escort arrived at the Broadway address, they were held in an anteroom for half an hour, and then admitted into a well-equipped office where a distinguished looking man, with a smooth face, wrote at a desk. General Falcon was presented to the Secretary of War of the United States, and his mission made known by his old friend, Mr. Kelley.

"Ah - Colombia!" said the Secretary, significantly, when he was made to understand; "I'm afraid there will be a little difficulty in that case. The President and I differ in our sympathies there. He prefers the established government, while I -" the secretary gave the General a mysterious but encouraging smile. "You, of course, know, General Falcon, that since the Tammany war, an act of Congress has been passed requiring all manufactured arms and *ammunition* exported from this country to pass through the War Department. Now, if I can do anything for you I will be glad to do so to oblige my old friend, Mr. Kelley. But it must be in absolute secrecy, as the President, as I have said, does not regard favourably the efforts of your revolutionary party in Colombia. I will have my orderly bring a list of the available arms now in the warehouse."

The Secretary struck a bell, and an orderly with the letters A. D. T. on his cap stepped promptly into the room.

"Bring me Schedule B of the small arms inventory," said the Secretary.

The orderly quickly returned with a printed paper. The Secretary studied it closely.

"I find," he said, "that in Warehouse 9, of Government stores, there is *shipment* of 2,000 stands of Winchester rifles that were ordered by the Sultan of Morocco, who forgot to send the cash with his order. Our rule is that legal-tender must be paid down at the time of purchase. My dear Kelley, your friend, General Falcon, shall have this lot of arms, if he desires it, at the manufacturer's price. And you will forgive me, I am sure, if I curtail our interview. I am expecting the Japanese Minister and Charles Murphy every moment!"

As one result of this interview, the General was deeply grateful to his *esteemed* friend, Mr. Kelley. As another, the

Shipment - *The act of sending of goods*
Auriferous - *Containing good*
Rude - *Crude, rough*
Gallant - *Smartly*

nimble Secretary of War was extremely busy during the next two days buying empty rifle cases and filling them with bricks, which were then stored in a *warehouse* rented for that purpose. As still another, when the General returned to the Hotel Espanol, Mrs. O'Brien went up to him, plucked a thread from his lapel, and said:

"Say, senor, I don't want to 'butt in,' but what does that monkey-faced, cat-eyed, rubber-necked tin horn tough want with you?"

"Sangre de mi vida!" exclaimed the General. "Impossible it is that you speak of my good friend, Senor Kelley."

"Come into the summer garden," said Mrs. O'Brien. "I want to have a talk with you."

Let us suppose that an hour has elapsed.

"And you say," said the General, "that for the sum of $18,000 can be purchased the *furnishment* of the house and the lease of one year with this garden so lovely - so *resembling* unto the *patios* of my cara Colombia?"

"And dirt cheap at that," sighed the lady.

"Ah, Dios!" breathed General Falcon. "What to me is war and politics? This spot is one *paradise*. My country it have other brave heroes to continue the fighting. What to me should be glory and the shooting of mans? Ah! no. It is here I have found one angel. Let us buy the Hotel Espanol and you shall be mine, and the money shall not be waste on guns." Mrs. O'Brien rested her blond pompadour against the shoulder of the Colombian *patriot*.

"Oh, senor," she sighed, happily, "ain't you terrible!"

Two days later was the time appointed for the delivery of the arms to the General. The boxes of supposed rifles were **stacked** in the rented warehouse, and the Secretary of War sat upon them, waiting for his friend Kelley to fetch the victim.

Mr. Kelley hurried, at the hour, to the Hotel Espanol. He found the General behind the desk adding up accounts.

"I have decide," said the General, "to buy not guns. I have to-day buy the insides of this hotel, and there shall be marrying of the General Perrico Ximenes Villablanca Falcon with la Madame O'Brien."

Mr. Kelley almost ***strangled***.

Nimble - *Light/agile in movement*
Warehouse - *A place in which goods are stored*
Patios - *Roofless inner court yard*
Stacked - *Piled*

Greatest Humour Stories

"Say, you old bald-headed bottle of shoe polish," he spluttered, "you're a *swindler* - that's what you are! You've bought a *boarding* house with money belonging to your *infernal* country, wherever it is."

"Ah," said the General, footing up a column, "that is what you call politics. War and revolution they are not nice. Yes. It is not best that one shall always follow Minerva. No. It is of quite desirable to keep hotels and be with that Juno - that ox-eyed Juno. Ah! what hair of the gold it is that she have!"

Mr. Kelley *choked* again.

"Ah, Senor Kelley!" said the General, feelingly and finally, "is it that you have never eaten of the corned *beef hash* that Madame O'Brien she make?"

Swindler - *To cheat*
Boarding - *Staying, residing*
Infernal - *Devilish*
Choked - *To stop the treath by squeezing*
Hash - *A dish of diced*

Food For Thought

The author, O.Henry is famous for surprise endings and this story is no exception. However, the best part of the story is when the General suggest Kelley to eat the corned beef hash that his love, Madame O'Brien makes. Explain the expressions and feelings of Kelley at that spur of the moment in your own words.

An Understanding

Q. 1. Who was General Falcon and from which country did he belong to? What was his business in New York that he had come for?
Ans. _____

Q. 2. Where did General falcon stay and who was Mrs. O'Brien? Describe how the General was infatuated by her blond (golden) hair and her beauty? Why do you think the author kept the name of the story 'The Gold that Glittered'?
Ans. _____

Q. 3. Who was Mr. Kelley and how did he plan to make a fool of General Falcon with the help of his friend and a well, known crook of New York Jimmy Dunn?
Ans. _____

Q. 4. How did Mr. Kelley become a fool himself and what did the General decide finally? What was Kelley's reaction to his decision?
Ans. _____

Greatest Humour Stories

HINDI LITERATURE

TALES & STORIES

All Books Fully Coloured

MUSIC (संगीत)

MAGIC & FACT (जादू एवं तथ्य)

MYSTERIES (रहस्य)

ACADEMIC BOOKS

All books available at **www.vspublishers.com**

www.ingramcontent.com/pod-product-compliance
Lightning Source LLC
Chambersburg PA
CBHW070329230426
43663CB00011B/2267